Controversial Issues in School Librarianship:

Divergent Perspectives

Nancy Everhart, Ph.D.

Library of Congress Cataloging-in-Publication Data

Everhart, Nancy.
  Controversial issues in school librarianship : divergent perspectives / by Nancy Everhart.
       p. cm.
  Includes bibliographical references and index.
  ISBN 1-58683-057-0
  1. School libraries--United States. 2. School librarians--United States. I. Title.
  Z675.S3E88 2003
  027.8--dc21
                                    2003012892

Published by Linworth Publishing, Inc.
480 East Wilson Bridge Road, Suite L
Worthington, Ohio 43085

Copyright © 2003 by Linworth Publishing, Inc.

All rights reserved. Purchasing this book entitles a librarian to reproduce activity sheets for use in the library within a school or entitles a teacher to reproduce activity sheets for single classroom use within a school. Other portions of the book (up to 15 pages) may be copied for staff development purposes within a single school. Standard citation information should appear on each page. The reproduction of any part of this book for an entire school or school system or for commercial use is strictly prohibited. No part of this book may be electronically reproduced, transmitted, or recorded without written permission from the publisher.

ISBN: 1-58683-057-0

5 4 3 2

Table of Contents

Acknowledgements vii

Introduction ix

Becoming a School Library Media Specialist 1
    Divergent Perspectives 2
        Certification 2
        Education for the Profession 4
        Distance Learning 7
        Teacher or Librarian? 9
    Questions for Discussion and Reflection 16
    Projects 17
    References 18
    Additional Information 19
    Web Sites 20

Professional Image 21
    Divergent Perspectives 22
        Librarians in the Media 22
        Perpetuating the Stereotype 26
        Education and Image 27
        The Invisible School Librarian 28
    Questions for Discussion and Reflection 30
    Projects 31
    References 32
    Additional Information 33
    Web Sites 33

Staffing the School Library Media Center 35
    Divergent Perspectives 37
        Staffing Mandates 37
        Shortage of School Library Media Specialists 39

Paraprofessionals 40
  Staffing and Technology 40
  Figure 1: State Mandates for School Library Media
      Specialists with Ratio of Students Per School
      Library Media Specialist 43
 Questions for Discussion and Reflection 45
 Projects 46
 References 47
 Additional Information 47
 Web Sites 48

Standards and Guidelines 49
 Divergent Perspectives 51
  Qualitative vs. Quantitative Standards 51
  Authority of Standards 52
  Communicating Standards 53
  Are Standards Realistic? 54
 Questions for Discussion and Reflection 56
 Projects 57
 References 58
 Web Sites 59

Collection Development 61
 Divergent Perspectives 62
  Responsibility for Selection 62
  Classroom Collections 63
  Curricular Needs and Personal Interests 64
  Censorship and Selection 65
  Funding for the Collection 67
 Questions for Discussion and Reflection 69
 Projects 70
 References 71
 Additional Information 71
 Web Sites 72

Computerized Reading Management Programs 73
 Divergent Perspectives 74
  Motivation and Rewards 74

Book Selection 76
　　　Library Collections and Budgets 76
　　　Staff Time 77
　　　Raising Reading Test Scores and Research 77
　　Questions for Discussion and Reflection 79
　　Projects 80
　　References 81
　　Additional Information 82
　　Web Sites 82

Scheduling 83
　　Divergent Perspectives 84
　　　Flexible Scheduling 84
　　　Fixed Scheduling 87
　　　Combining Fixed and Flexible Scheduling 90
　　　Block Scheduling 91
　　Questions for Discussion and Reflection 94
　　Projects 95
　　References 96
　　Additional Information 97
　　Web Sites 98

Facilities 99
　　Divergent Perspectives 100
　　　Are School Library Media Centers Necessary? 100
　　　Extended Hours 101
　　　Combined School-Public Libraries 103
　　　The School Library Media Center in Year-Round Schools ...106
　　　School Library Media Centers Incorporating Design
　　　　Ideas from Bookstores 108
　　　Homeschoolers 109
　　　Furnishings 111
　　Questions for Discussion and Reflection 113
　　Projects 114
　　References 115
　　Additional Information 116
　　Web Sites 117

Table of Contents / v

Virtual/Digital School Libraries ... 119
- Divergent Perspectives ... 120
    - Roles of the Virtual School Library and Virtual School Librarian ... 120
    - Accessing the Virtual School Library ... 123
    - 24–7 Access ... 124
    - State Digital Libraries ... 124
    - The Internet Is No Substitute for a Library ... 125
    - eBooks ... 126
    - Measuring Use ... 129
- Questions for Discussion and Reflection ... 131
- Projects ... 132
- References ... 133
- Additional Information ... 134
- Web Sites ... 135

Glossary ... 137

Index ... 143

About the Author ... 150

Acknowledgements

The author would like to thank two dear friends, Kay Bishop and Betty Morris, whose brainstorming led to the conceptualization and publication of this book. I am grateful to colleagues at the University of Hawaii Library and Information Science Program, Vi Harada, Péter Jacsó, and Diane Nahl, who arranged for me to teach a course in the summer of 2002 based on the issues presented here. Class members, Sandra Kugisaki-Ongie, Susan Smith, Gail Miyashita, Jamie Young, Jennifer Simon, Diana Morales, Elizabeth Kaneshiro, Jon Fletcher, Shelly Tanaka, Kristi Atalig, and Amber Collins were instrumental in providing input into the draft manuscript. Aya Asano, my research assistant, was extremely helpful. Colleague, Bella Weinberg, imparted her indexing wisdom. My friend, newspaper editor George Taylor, spent countless hours improving various versions. I extend special thanks to Linworth staff, Marlene Woo-Lun and Judi Repman, for their encouragement. And always, my gratitude goes to Harry, Drew, and Keith Everhart, who support all my endeavors.

Introduction

This book presents pros and cons on many issues that are controversial in school librarianship. One might ask—what could be controversial in such a refined and intellectual profession? There are numerous concerns. What is the optimal education for a school library media specialist? Should school library media centers purchase popular materials? eBooks? What is the impact on the library media program when there is access to electronic resources in classrooms and at home? *Accelerated Reader*? Fixed or flexible scheduling? Can we learn anything from bookstores? These, and other issues, have advocates and critics. What is unique about the approach used to discuss controversial issues here is that there is not an attempt to be politically correct, but to honestly and sincerely view the issues from all perspectives.

There are many more topics that might be considered controversial in the school library media field that did not find their way into this book. In order to form a focus for what has been included several steps were taken. First, an effort was made to concentrate on issues that are national in scope, thus having the potential to reach all school library media specialists. Second, issues were chosen that provoke strong opinions in people but have no right or wrong points of view. And third, there are controversial topics (filtering, for example) that were intentionally omitted due to the fact that official laws or policies are in place that are either under attack by those outside the profession, or for which there is no current recourse.

Information and opinions were gathered from a variety of sources —research reports, articles in professional journals, listservs, Web sites, conference presentations, and classroom and personal discussions. That is not to say that equal weight has been given to listserv postings and formal research, but in many instances, the topics are so new or so controversial, little has appeared in the professional literature about them.

The readings found here can be used to introduce students in school library media preparation programs to issues in the field. The discussion questions, projects, and sources for further information, as well as a glossary, make it useful as a textbook for beginners. Current school library media specialists will be interested in the new twists and opposing viewpoints on themes that have continuously been debated such as scheduling, image, certification, collection development, and computerized reading programs. Of further interest to practitioners is recent dialogue on virtual school libraries, unique uses of facilities, and staffing. The pros and cons, advantages and disadvantages, research, and sources of further information can assist professionals in tasks such as gathering background data for grant proposals, supporting program changes with administrators, and improving job performance. Woven throughout the book are threads dealing with political realities of the job as well as workable strategies to overcome obstacles that accompany the issues discussed. It is not the goal of this book to promote consensus on these topics, but to encourage dialogue and further exploration.

Becoming a School Library Media Specialist

Becoming a school library media specialist involves two distinct processes—education and certification. Each state has unique requirements for certification, which are fulfilled in part by educational preparation. The current breakdown (Lau, 2002) of the educational background for school library media specialists is:

- ▶ M.L.S. from an ALA-accredited school 39%
- ▶ Master's degree 22%
- ▶ College graduate 17%
- ▶ M.L.S. from a non-ALA-accredited school 13%
- ▶ Currently enrolled in M.L.S. program 4%
- ▶ Ph.D. 2%
- ▶ Some college 2%
- ▶ High school graduate 1%

Although various types of education and professional development provide adequate preparation for the duties of a school library media specialist, the professional organization, the American Association of School Librarians (AASL) has prescribed guidelines. The AASL "Position Statement on Preparation of School Library Media Specialists" states:

> School library media specialists have a broad undergraduate education with a liberal arts background and hold a master's degree or equivalent from a program that combines academic and professional preparation in library and information

science, education, management, media, communications theory, and technology. The academic program of study includes some directed field experience in a library media program, coordinated by a faculty member in cooperation with an experienced library media specialist. Library media specialists meet state certification requirements for both the library media specialist and professional educator classifications. While there may be many practicing library media specialists who have only an undergraduate degree and whose job performance is outstanding, the master's degree is considered the entry-level degree for the profession. The graduate degree is earned at colleges and universities whose programs are accredited by appropriate bodies such as the American Library Association (ALA), the National Council for the Accreditation of Teacher Education (NCATE), or state education agencies (AASL, 1992).

Divergent Perspectives

Partly because of the discrepancies stemming from unique requirements for certification across states, debates rage. What is the best preparation to become a school library media specialist? Divergent perspectives abound in the matters of education, focus, prior background, and type of educational degree.

■ Certification

The issue of certification is addressed first because state certification requirements dictate the type of library education necessary. Certification as a school library media specialist is determined by a credentialing agency within each state's department of education. If you obtain certification in one state, it is no guarantee that you will be certified in another. Differences exist in the following areas: title of the credential, educational program, experience, and required tests. Patsy Perritt's articles, published bi-annually in *School Library Journal*, contain valuable information about state requirements, variations, and contacts information for school library media certification. One of her best articles appears in the June 2000 issue and is appropriately titled,

"Getting Certified in 50 States: The Latest Requirements for School Librarians."

The school library media credential can be a certificate or an endorsement. An endorsement usually implies an add-on to an existing teaching certificate, which requires less coursework than a full degree. Titles of the credential or endorsement also vary between states. They include: school library media specialist, library science, library media teacher, librarian/media specialist, school media librarian, learning resources specialist, educational media specialist, and media generalist. A handful of states also distinguish between endorsements as an elementary or a secondary school library media specialist in their requirements.

The educational program that is necessary for school library media specialist certification ranges from requiring a master's degree from an approved program in addition to a teaching credential in New Jersey, to a bachelor's degree with 16 hours in library media education in North Dakota (Perritt, 2000). Variations exist as to whether or not the state-credentialing agency requires candidates to take explicit courses, demonstrate competencies, or complete a program approved by that state's department of education. Courses are often specified in the areas of administration, technology, cataloging, reference, literature, selection, and field experience.

The swiftest routes to endorsement are in Arizona, Florida, Mississippi, and Missouri. There, candidates need simply pass a credentialing test. Arizona and Florida use a state exam; Mississippi and Missouri utilize the national Praxis II exam for library media specialists developed by Educational Testing Service. From 1992–2000, teachers in Texas could take the state test called the Examination for Certification of Educators in Texas, or the ExCET, for endorsement as a school librarian. The results were disastrous. A district coordinator of school libraries commented on 15 teachers who were put into libraries after passing the state test: "There are two components to any library program. One is serving patrons and getting them resource materials. The second is librarianship and management, and that's where they were absolutely clueless. They didn't know how to order materials, what resources to go to, or how to meet needs as far as district goals are concerned" (Glick, 1999, p. 16). The state director of library services added that she received countless calls from exam-certified librarians who didn't know how to run their libraries. On-the-job floundering and lack of a realization of the difficult role they had assumed contributed to Texas stopping the practice (Glick, 2000).

Once on the job, three types of certification apply: provisional; permanent; and emergency. Everyone enters the profession with a provisional (sometimes referred to as initial) certification. In order for certification to become permanent, years of experience, and in some states, more coursework, is needed. Again, each state's requirements are different. Emergency certification is just that — when no one with matching certification can be found to fill a job opening, a school can hire someone certified in another teaching field. That person must agree to work toward certification as a school library media specialist, usually at the rate of six credits per year. This is becoming more and more commonplace in the field because of the nationwide shortage of qualified school library media specialists (Everhart, 2000).

National Board certification (National Board for Professional Teaching Standards, 2003), another new type of certification, is available to school library media specialists. National Board certification is appropriate for accomplished teachers who have completed at least three years of teaching (Coatney, 2000). National Board certification is voluntary and should not be confused with initial certification, which all teachers must satisfy for entry into the profession. More and more states are beginning to recognize national certification as applicable to their state so recertification isn't necessary for those people who change state residency. As an added advantage, employers and states offer salary incentive packages to teachers who become nationally certified. Although the certification/assessment process is expensive ($2,300) and will take most of the school year to complete, many states offer support programs. Information about state and district support is available at the NBPTS (2003) Web site.

■ Education for the Profession

Once you've made the decision to become a school library media specialist, answering the following questions will clarify the direction of your library education.

First, are you knowledgeable about the certification requirements in the state where you plan to work? The information provided by Patsy Perritt's articles includes Web sites and phone numbers for each state's credentialing agency where you can confirm the requirements.

Second, will the preparation for initial certification also count toward permanent certification, a master's degree, and future pay raises? For example, in North Dakota certification is at the undergraduate level with 16 semester hours in library media education. Although these 16 semester hours and an additional ten credits apply to permanent certification, they will not apply to pay raises — only graduate courses count toward salary increases. In Florida, 30 graduate credits apply toward certification, but just 36 are needed for a master's degree. Simply put, it may be worthwhile to work toward a master's degree. In some states like New York and Wisconsin, no decision is necessary — a master's degree is a requirement for permanent certification.

Third, do you definitely plan to work in school libraries in the same state for your entire career? Again, the answer to this question narrows down the choices of which type of master's degree you will need. Obtaining a master's degree from a graduate school accredited by the American Library Association (ALA) is necessary for employment in public, academic, and special libraries, but not schools. An ALA degree provides a broad perspective of all types of libraries and also allows for specialization in school media, usually obtained by taking a school media "track" within the program. Some school library media specialists want the flexibility of an ALA degree so they can work in their local public or college library in the summers or on weekends to earn extra money, or they may plan to work in another type of library after retirement. If you are going for a master's in librarianship, make certain that you know exactly what you are looking for and what you want to be able to do with it. Sometimes, school library media specialists find out after spending thousands of dollars and countless hours of time, that an ALA degree is necessary for employment in public and academic libraries (Everhart, 1998).

If working in another type of library is not a concern, a master's degree from a school accredited by the National Council for Accreditation of Teacher Education (NCATE) is an option. NCATE programs offer master's degrees in school library media, learning resources specialist, educational media specialist, and others more focused on the school library media field (AASL, 2001). Divergent perspectives, such as the one that follows, exist about which type of master's degree is more appropriate for school library media specialists:

Dear Fellow Librarians,

I have read the discussions about degrees needed to be a librarian, the differences between school and public librarianship, and why or why not a librarian "needs" an M.L.S. I guess my concern is that we are devouring each other instead of building up the profession of librarianship. It appears that we are judging our fellow librarians not on the job they are doing but on the degree they hold. Is this the message we want to send? In my state, teachers get a BS in Education with a concentration in their area, be it English, math, or library science and are certified K–12, K–6, 7–12, etc. based on what they have taken in college. You then have six years to get 24 more credits. Usually these lead to a master's degree or another field of certification. I student taught on all three levels, elementary, junior high, and senior high and graduated with a BS in education, certified K–12 in library science. I have more than 50 credits past my original degree and am taking my fifth graduate class in computers starting tonight.

It seems to me that the quality of the job the person does, as well as the willingness to keep current and up to date, is far more important than a piece of paper. Some years ago I had a substitute librarian with a M.L.S. who was scared of high school students, didn't want to teach any classes, and couldn't understand why she couldn't just catalog books all day. Needless to say, we didn't use her very often. My point is that we must work together to build librarianship in all forms and in all kinds of libraries and not denigrate any fellow librarian who may have taken a different path than we did. You do not often hear doctors disparage other doctors, or lawyers disparage other lawyers. To build up the profession of librarianship you do not tear down other librarians (Bickel, 1998).

Finally, you have to locate the nearest education facility with the coursework you need. Traditionally, master's degree candidates in the school library media field are already working full time and may also have families. Bound geographically, their options are dictated by traveling to the closest university with a library media program. These programs are spread unevenly throughout the country and often not within driving distance of many prospective students.

■ Distance Learning

In response to the nationwide shortage of school library media specialists, distance learning alternatives have become available. During the past few years, an alphabetical listing of distance learning programs has been accessible on the ALA (2001) Web site. Mansfield University, a regionally accredited institution with an online curriculum, is unique in that it is geared strictly to potential school library media specialists. The growth and popularity of online library degrees has resulted in a listing in *U.S. News and World Report* (2003) of the "Online Graduate Programs: Library Science." Program characteristics such as degrees offered, number of students, visits to campus required, access speed, technical help, and cost per credit hour are available for comparison purposes. In addition to online curricula, other distance learning options include summer institutes run by state departments of education and universities, courses encompassing television delivery, and traveling instructors.

Christine Jenkins (2000), a professor who teaches via distance education for the University of Illinois Graduate School of Library Information Science, admits she was initially skeptical that an online class could effectively create a community of learners. In a classroom environment, students learn from each other as well as the instructor and the class as a whole becomes a great deal more than the sum of its parts and she wondered if this environment could be replicated in cyberspace. Surprisingly, she discovered that the course went very well and despite its "virtual" twist, it feet completely real. Jenkins attributes the online course's success to a component of real-time interaction, the support of technical experts, and a library "boot camp" where students spent two weeks on campus during the summer to learn technical skills and form personal ties. She advises students choosing a distance program to consider the following:

1. Is it possible to earn an entire degree online? If not, how many credits must you complete on campus? What classes are available to distance students?
2. Do tenured or tenure-track faculty teach distance courses?

3. What computer technology — hardware, software, and technical support — will you need? Could your workplace provide access to any of this?
4. What technological support and resources does the school provide? Is technical support readily available? Can they support Macs? PCs? Is there an 800 number?
5. What library services and resources does the program provide? Do courses make use of online reserve readings? What about delivery of hard copy, interlibrary loan, or photocopies via mail or fax? What reference services are provided?
6. What is the mix of synchronous vs. asynchronous instruction? Are you available for regularly scheduled class meetings, or do you need the flexibility of classes you can take on your own time?
7. How much time is required on campus?

For students pursuing an online degree who do not live in the state where the university is located, certification is another consideration. Potential students should contact the credentialing agency in their state department of education to ensure that the online degree will be acceptable.

Students currently enrolled in online library education programs shared the pros and cons of this type of learning on various LM_NET posts.

PROS
- it provides access to a degree that would not otherwise be possible;
- you can "go to school" at your convenience;
- the use of the Internet and the computer are learning experiences in themselves;
- some instructors allow you adapt assignments to your needs;
- instructors are always available; and
- feedback is constant.

CONS
- there is a lack of personal interaction with classmates and faculty;
- you have to be a self-starter who is not afraid to ask questions if you have problems;

- ▶ sometimes the technology fails;
- ▶ out-of-state tuition is required for public universities if you don't live in that state; and
- ▶ it's more work.

■ Teacher or Librarian?

School library media specialists are unique in that they are a blend of teacher and librarian. The focus of education for school librarianship is often debated—should it be on the teacher component or the librarian component? Perhaps nowhere was this debate more public and heated than between Dr. Keith Swigger, dean of the School of Library and Information Studies at Texas Woman's University, and Dr. Michael Eisenberg, director of the School of Library and Information Science at the University of Washington, both of whom are widely recognized and respected in the profession. The debate began with an opinion piece in *School Library Journal* by Dr. Swigger (1999) titled, "Librarian, Teach Thyself: It's time for school librarians to focus on librarianship—not teaching." Dr. Eisenberg took issue with Swigger's analysis and a rebuttal appeared in *The Book Report*. Both sides are reprinted here with permission.

> **Librarian, Teach Thyself: It's time for school librarians to focus on librarianship—not teaching.**
>
> *Reprinted with permission from* School Library Journal, *October 1999, p. 45.*
>
> Does anybody want to be a librarian? The statistics say hardly any college students aspire to join the field. Librarianship is a "discovery career" to which people turn when Plan A in their lives doesn't work out.
>
> At the same time, some librarians use rhetoric and promote strategies that say they don't really want to be librarians, but, rather, want to do some other profession's work. Corporate librarians want to be knowledge asset managers. Public librarians want to be bookstore managers. Academic librarians want to be university faculty. And school librarians want to be teachers—just not in the classroom, thank you.

Rather than focus on providing service—which some find demeaning—many librarians in the "information literacy" movement would train those who should be our clients to serve themselves. That way librarians can do something else: teach classes, design curricula, or sit in the seats of educational power and control.

Why doesn't anyone want to be a librarian? A fundamental reason may be that we have never treated school librarianship as a profession in its own right. It's been a hybrid of teaching and librarianship, with, in many cases, a more modest length and level of preparation than other branches of the profession. We act as if school librarianship had no separate identity, no unique contributions to make, little knowledge to master. Eighty years ago it may have been desirable that school librarians be prepared primarily as teachers. But in our time, students' needs call for a differentiation of roles.

A profession's legitimacy rests on three basic elements: its practitioners' unique mastery of useful skills; its effective delivery of services; and society's recognition that the profession has both the authority and competence to solve important problems. A profession focuses on its own expertise. It is responsive to its client's needs. And it differentiates itself from other professions.

I think it's time we professionalize school librarianship. Why? Because children would be better served. Knowledge and information systems, from books to computers to networks, are demanding. But they are only tools, they change frequently, and understanding how to use them should not be the goal or end in itself. If librarians would focus on serving their clients instead of trying to help them master information systems, we would conserve our users' time and attention, both of which are irreplaceable resources. We err if we claim that what librarians do is what everyone should learn.

How can we professionalize school librarianship? Here's what we should do: Separate the certification of librarians from that of teachers, and directly credential school librarianship. In most states, the primary certification for school librarians is based on the qualifications as a teacher, not a librarian.

Revise the professional preparation system to include longer programs of study — a few introductory courses won't suffice. Abandon the old model of tacked-on, post-baccalaureate courses available only to teachers. Stop denigrating school librarians' work, stop apologizing for it, and stop clamoring for the right to do someone else's work instead. Librarians are librarians; teachers are teachers — different names, different work. School librarians now need more expertise to cope with changes in the infrastructure of knowledge and information systems with the variety of pressures a diverse society generates.

Develop a stronger service orientation. Service is the touchstone of all professions, and librarians should provide library services: setting up and maintaining complex collections and electronic knowledge systems, answering reference questions, delivering resources to students and teachers, and knowing the collection to advise readers.

Finally, abandon zealotry and hyperbole. Information isn't life. It isn't even power. The library isn't the center of the school — it's an integral part of a system. Relax. Librarianship does offer opportunities to engage in decent work, to be helpful, and to participate in intellectually challenging experiences. That's a lot.

Dr. Keith Swigger
Dean
School of Library and Information Studies
Texas Woman's University

An Open Letter to Dr. Keith Swigger Regarding His Piece in *School Library Journal*, October 1999.

Reprinted with permission from The Book Report, *January–February 2000, pp. 44–45.*

Dear Keith,

I'm writing in response to your October 1999 "Make Your Point" in *School Library Journal*. First, let me thank you for once again raising these important questions. It's healthy for any profession to respond to questions about its purpose and value. This is particularly appropriate in a world that's being turned upside-down, where even traditional professions such as law and medicine are undergoing fundamental changes.

Some of what you say is right on target: school librarianship should be consistently "professionalized" throughout the country through rigorous education and certification programs on the master's level. But, most of the rest of what you say is absolutely wrong.

School librarians have no identity crisis. We have a widely accepted mission statement adopted by AASL over 10 years ago and recently reaffirmed in the new standards: "The mission of the library media program is to ensure that students and staff are effective users of ideas and information" (AASL, AECT Information Power, 1998, 1999). And, school librarians know how to fulfill this mission: by (1) providing a full range of essential services (including resources provision, access, reference and information service, and reading guidance and literature appreciation) and (2) teaching essential information and technology skills. School librarians don't have to choose between two equally important functions — service and instruction — rather they are leaders in integrating them. School library professionals are working hard to improve their ability to deliver on both — through pre-service and continuing professional development, by taking advantage of the opportunities afforded by new technologies, and by expanding the reach of library programs in schools through collaboration with technology specialists, classroom teachers, and administrators.

Interestingly, in my recent work with other types of librarians — including academic, public, medical, law, and special — I find that they, too, are increasingly recognizing the importance of instruction and training in meeting the needs of their constituents. In fact, in our revision of the master's curriculum at the School of Library and Information Science at the University of Washington, we have added a new required course for all library students: Instruction & Training in Library and Information Environments. This course has been met with universal support from professionals in the field, faculty, and students in our program. People no longer enter the school library profession to escape the classroom. On the contrary, they are drawn by the opportunity to work with students in flexible learning environments, to make the connection between students and information, resources, and literature, and to reach across the school rather than focusing on one class or subject area. You state that a profession's legitimacy rests on three elements. School library work meets all three: school librarians have mastered the essential skills of providing information services, of building and managing physical and virtual libraries, and of teaching information and technology skills; school librarians are increasingly able to meet the needs of students through delivery of services — including provision of resources and skills instruction; and the school and broader community are increasingly recognizing the importance of library and information work in schools and the unique and important role of the school librarian.

    In my very first class in library school, Bill Katz raised the same issue of service vs. instruction. He made a strong case for not teaching everyone to be a librarian; that we had unique skills and should use those skills to provide services to patrons and not worry about teaching them how to do our job. I now know that this argument oversimplifies the situation. There's a continuum from self-service to full-service. Should the public turn to a librarian every time they have the simplest information need? No, in the same way that people shouldn't turn to a doctor when they have a small cut or scrape or cold. But, they should contact a medical (or library) professional when they have a problem that requires unique, professional-level services. Furthermore, we now realize that we are not just talking about skills related to finding information. People need to be able to figure out just what they need in the first place, and then how to use, apply, and pull together information from a range of sources to meet that need. These are essential information skills, and it is only logical that the primary information professional in the school — the school librarian — should be responsible for ensuring that students learn these skills. At the same time, school librarians cannot teach every aspect of every information skill; this requires a collaborative effort involving classroom teachers, other educators and even parents. However, school librarians are the most qualified educators to plan and coordinate the integrated information skills instructional program.

Finally, you urge school librarians to "abandon zealotry and hyperbole," because information isn't life, and it isn't even power. Wrong. Information is essential to almost every endeavor in life—to learning, various work activities, even recreation. Even football, something of great importance in the state of Texas, can be viewed as a contest of competing information systems. Do you really believe that it really makes no difference—in terms of success in school, business, public service, personal well-being—whether or not a person is skilled in finding, evaluating, and using information?

You say that, "Librarians won't save the world." I say, "Why not?" I believe in the value of information for decision-making, learning, and helping people to achieve their aspirations. Furthermore, I believe that the full range of information skills (including the ability to define an information need, to select and access sources, to extract relevant information, to combine information to resolve the need, and to evaluate effectiveness and efficiency) are part of the new basics of K–12 education. I sometimes kid my friends in the medical profession that all they do is to patch kids up so that we can do the really important work—to help them to develop their minds. Okay, I'll back down; medicine is important too. But, in my mind, there's nothing any more important than what we do as school librarians: ensuring that students are effective users of ideas and information.

Sincerely,

Mike Eisenberg
Library Media Educator
Director and Professor
School of Library and Information Science
University of Washington

The paths to becoming a professional school library media specialist vary in length and emphasis of coursework as well as convenience. Although state certification requirements limit the direction of that path to a point, options are available to all who seek library education. Because the job is multi-faceted as well as constantly changing, you must continue to educate yourself throughout your career.

Questions for Discussion and Reflection

1. What is your reaction to the Swigger-Eisenberg debate? Which do you think is a better background for a school library media specialists — librarian or teacher? Why?

2. If you could design an exam that allows someone to become a school library media specialist upon passing, what areas or skills would you measure?

3. What does "professionalize" mean? How can school librarianship be professionalized?

4. Discuss the reasons why you want to become, or did become, a school library media specialist.

5. Have you taken any courses online? Discuss your experiences. If you haven't, would you like to? Explain why or why not.

Projects

1. Survey at least ten school library media specialists in your immediate area. Ask them what type of education they have using the categories from the *School Library Journal* (Perritt, 2000) survey. Choose some to interview and learn the path they took and the advantages and disadvantages of their education. If possible, visit the libraries of librarians with different educational backgrounds and determine if you think this makes a difference in their program and philosophy.

2. Access the Web sites of three schools in "Online Graduate Programs: Library Science" (*U.S. News and World Report*, 2003). Explore the degree characteristics and make a decision on which program you would like to attend and explain why.

3. Complete one of the certification activities for school library media specialists at the NBPTS Web site

References

American Association of School Librarians. (1992). Position statement in preparation of school library media specialists. Retrieved Jouly 7, 2003, from<www.ala.org/Content/NavigationMenu/AASL/Professional_Tools10/Postion_Statements/AASL_Position_Statement_on_Preparation_of_School_Library_Media_Specialists.htm>.

American Association of School Librarians. (2001, October 30). *School library media education programs in NCATE-accredited educational units.* Retrieved July 7, 2003, from<www.ala.org/aaslTemplate.cfm?Section=School Library Media Education Programs&Templates=/ContentManagement/ContentDisplay.cfm&ContentID=20297>.

American Library Association. Office for Accreditation. (2001). ALA accredited LIS programs that provide distance education opportunities. Retrieved September 30, 2002 from <www.ala.org/alaorg/oa/disted.html>.

Bickel, J. (1998, January 27). Librarian certification and training. Message posted to<www.askeric.org/Virtual/Listserv_Archives/LM_NET-pre2000/1998/Jan_1998/msg01563.html>.

Coatney, S. (2000, December). School library media specialists and the National Board for Professional Teaching Standards. S*chool Library Media Activities Monthly, 17* (4), 24–25.

Eisenberg, M. (2000, Jan/Feb). An open letter to Dr. Keith Swigger regarding his piece in "School Library Journal." *Book Report, 18* (4), 44–45.

Everhart, N. (1998, May 22). HIT: Why get your degree? Message posted to <www.askeric.org/plweb-cgi/fastweb?getdoc+listservs+LM_NET-1998+12748+0+wAAA+why%26get%26your%26degree>.

Everhart, N. (2000, September). According to the latest research, the shortage of school librarians is becoming a national crisis. *School Library Journal, 46* (9) 58–61.

Glick, A. (1999, October). A test for Texas librarians. *School Library Journal, 45* (10), 16–17.

Glick, A. (2000, November). Raising the bar. *School Library Journal, 46* (11), 17.

Jenkins, C. (2000, February). Far out learning. *School Library Journal, 46* (2), 46–9.

Lau, D. (2002, May). Got clout? *School Library Journal, 48* (5), 40–45.

National Board for Professional Teaching Standards. (2003). Standards: Early childhood through young adulthood/library media. Retrieved July 7, 2003, from <www.nbpts.org/standards/ng_ov_ecya_lm.cfm>.

Perritt, P. (2000, June). Getting certified in 50 states: The latest requirements for school librarians. *School Library Journal, 46* (6), 50–72.

Swigger, K. (1999, October). Librarian, teach thyself: It's time for school librarians to focus on librarianship—not teaching. *School Library Journal, 45* (10), 45.

U.S. News and World Report. (2002). Online graduate programs: library science. Retrieved July 7, 2003 from <www.usnews.com/usnews/edu/elearning/tables/lib_reg_prof.htm>.

Additional Information

Barron, D. (1990). Research related to the education of school library media specialists. In Woolls, B. (Ed.), *Research of school library media centers: Papers of the Treasure Mountain Research Retreat, Park City, Utah, October 17–18, 1989* (pp. 215–230). Castle Rock, CO: Hi Willow Research and Publishers.

Callison, D., & Tilley, C. (2001). Preparing school library media specialists for the new century: Results of a survey. *Journal of Education for Library and Information Science, 42* (3), 220–27.

Everhart, N. (2002, June). Filling the void. *School Library Journal, 48* (6), 44–49.

Fallis, D., & Fricke, M. (1999, October 15). Not by library school alone. *Library Journal, 124* (17), 42–43.

Glick, A. (2002, April). The first all-virtual library school. *School Library Journal, 48* (4), 54–56.

Harada, V. (1996). School library media preparation programs in ALA-accredited schools. *Journal of Education for Library and Information Science, 37* (3), 210–28.

Hopkins, D. M. (1999). Issues in the education of school library media specialists. Retrieved October 2 from: <www.ala.org/congress.hopkins_print.html>.

Shannon, D. (2002). Education and competencies of school library media specialists: A review of the literature. *School Library Media Research*, 5, <www.ala.org/Content/NavigationMenu/AASL/Publications_and_Journals/School_Library_Media_Research/Contents1/Volume_5_(2002)/Shannon.htm

Web Sites

ALA/AASL Standards For Initial Programs for School Library Media Specialist Preparation
<www.ala.org/Content/NavigationMenu/AASL/Education_and_Careers1/School_Library_Media_Education_Programs/ala-aasl_slma2003.pdf>
Detailed performance-based competencies are described for standards related to functioning as a professional school library media specialist. Competencies are presented in rubric format at the levels of unacceptable, acceptable, and target.

ALA Directory of Accredited LIS Master's Programs
<www.ala.org/alaorg/oa/lisdir.html>
An alphabetical, state-by-state listing is provided, followed by a province-by-province listing of Canadian programs. An index by institution is also available. The listings are followed by "Guidelines for Choosing a Master's Program in Library and Information Studies."

School Librarianship as a Career
<www.ala.org/aasl/resources/career.html>
Links to national resources, education programs, state certification requirements, and recruitment information produced by the American Association of School Librarians.

Professional Image

Professional image has been a continuing issue for all types of librarians. The public has a stereotype of librarians, perpetuated by popular media, which has been hard to overcome. Likenesses abound from the prim and proper *Marian the Librarian* in *The Music Man* to Donna Reed in *It's a Wonderful Life*, whose fate is to succumb to life as a spinster librarian, complete with glasses and bun, if Jimmy Stewart had never been born.

Norman Stevens (1988) reviewed stereotypical images in three major library journals from 1980 to 1986 and concluded that "as a profession we are no closer to any resolution of how to deal with this most important and vexatious of all professional questions than we were in 1876, 1907, or 1962. The issue of our image will persist and will undoubtedly be no closer to resolution in another decade or two than it is now. We will simply have a more extensive body of folklore and literature to deal with" (p. 825). Stevens' predictions, unfortunately, held true as evidenced when a group of 100 people were asked, "What are typical librarian characteristics?" on a recent "Family Feud" game show. They answered: 1) quiet; 2) mean or stern; 3) single/unmarried; 4) stuffy; and 5) wears glasses.

Not all depictions of librarians have been negative. In the 1957 film *Desk Set*, Spencer Tracy is hired to install a new computer in the reference department of a TV network that is set to replace the librarians played by Katharine Hepburn, Joan Blondell, Dina Merrill, and Sue Randall. The intelligent and attractive women proceed to outsmart the computer at several turns. A more recent film, *Party Girl*, features a striking twenty-something whose penchant for partying gets her evicted from her apartment. Her aunt gets her a job in the New York Public Library system where she realizes her spirited personality and talents make her the perfect librarian (Rarish, 2003).

Although the majority of librarians portrayed as negative stereotypes in the movies, on television, and in print ads are not typically school librarians, the image transfers to them. The reality is that the other teachers in the building classically think of the school librarian as a librarian—not as a teacher.

Divergent Perspectives

School library media specialists' professional image is influenced by how all librarians are represented in the media, both positively and negatively. Divergent perspectives as to whether the preponderance of stereotypes may serve to attract or detract potential members of the profession flourish. Education of school library media specialists, as well as administrators' indifference to school library media programs that relate to the issue of image, will be discussed in this chapter.

■ Librarians in the Media

Librarian characters have often been used in advertising and entertainment. In the pre-Internet days, *American Libraries*, the official journal of the American Library Association, ran a media watch column, "Our Image: How They're Seeing Us," which was published as often as people sent in examples of negative or positive media images.

> Readers were encouraged to send in protests to the offending parties. There were many, many negative examples, including an eyeglass ad where three photos of a drab looking woman were accompanied by three insulting captions: Edna Blue Rinse—Suburban!, Betty Bland—the washed out woman, while the third reads, "Yes, I'm the Chief Librarian." However, after a while, ad campaigns began to run more positive images of librarians, sometimes by corporations. In 1987, an ad agency ran a corporate image ad focusing on its special librarians. "Sandra's got connections," ran the caption accompanying

a photo of an sophisticated woman wearing a smart suit (no glasses! nice haircut!). She is described as a "charming, efficient, and very smart librarian." Why has the column become such a rarity in 1990s? The image may have improved, but another factor that has been at work according to the editor is: "We've screamed pretty loudly. Now there are not as many violations. The worst one happened last year in a computer ad which showed librarians in a row looking like they were goose-stepping and saying "Shhh." She added, "There are all kinds of librarians, from preservationists to pop culture habitués. There's an evolution in the image of the librarian. I think the image is changing a great deal" (Marinelli & Baker, 2003).

A replacement for the "How They're Seeing Us" column is the Internet Public Library's (2003) links to "Image of Librarians Resources." One timely link, "Librarians In The Movies: An Annotated Filmography" (Rarish, 2003) is comprehensive. According to its creator, "This filmography is an ongoing attempt to expand our collective memory, to find a more comprehensive and defensible basis for our acceptance or rejection of the "typical movie librarian"—whatever we think he or she is. It lists over 400 Hollywood (and a few foreign) productions that in some significant or memorable way include a library or librarian." Descriptions are provided for the library settings and the librarians. A few school libraries and school librarians make the list:

- ▶ *Big Bully* (1996). Rick Moranis comes back to teach at his old high school. As he walks down the hall to his classroom on the first day, he passes the library, peers in, and sees his old librarian still sitting at her desk, just as he remembers her. He walks in, reminds her who he is, tells her how meaningful the library was in his life... and she pulls out an overdue slip and tells him how much he owes on a book he still has out!
- ▶ *Christine* (1983). A scene early in the film portrays a confrontation between the "hero" and the school librarian over talking.
- ▶ *The Prime of Miss Jean Brodie* (1969). Two girls are in the school library composing a letter. Their giggling distracts the librarian, a rather sour sort who is checking out books. She walks over to see what they're up to, shushes them, and

eventually chases them out of the library. The girls slip the letter in a book, but the librarian finds it and declares, "This is a library!"
- ▶ *Rome Adventure* (1962). Suzanne Pleshette, a pretty librarian in an American girls' school, goes to Rome to learn about love, and does.
- ▶ *The Breakfast Club* (1985). Five students serve detention time in the library. One kid switches around a bunch of cards in the card catalog, another tears out pages from a volume of Moliere.
- ▶ *Carrie* (1976). Sissy Spacek searches through her high school library looking for books on mental telepathy.

Perhaps the most positive image of a school librarian in the media is Rupert Giles, on the TV show, *Buffy the Vampire Slayer*.

> Giles, this wily and attractive professional, is our hero librarian: a pop culture idol whose love of books and devotion to research hold the key to saving the universe—every week...
>
> It is a heady experience for any profession to find itself an integral part of a wildly popular TV series. How much more so for librarians, who have been bedeviled with a poor public image at least since the nineteenth century. Giles of course moves across the stereotype in other, not necessarily positive ways—he is both male and technologically inept. Giles is tweedy, occasionally befuddled, and very wise, with a certain amount of darkness in his own past. He dropped out of Oxford to pursue magicks, but then moved to the British Library, and thence to Sunnydale where duty called him. He comes from a family of Watchers, reads a number of languages, and, until her untimely death, had a passionate relationship with the Romany technopagan computer instructor, Jenny Calendar.
>
> We have a librarian model who is elegant, deeply educated, well if fussily dressed, handsome, and charged with eroticism. In a world of teens where parents rarely make an appearance, he is a stable, friendly, and supportive adult. He stands by Buffy even when the powers that be require him to step down. He lives the faith that answers can be found, and

most often found in the pages of a book.
Giles is icon and image for us; in him we see our quotidian struggles to provide the right information and the right data resolved into a cosmic drama with the forces of darkness, some of which are extremely attractive, by the way. We love Giles because at last we have a pop image for our uneasy relationship with dark and light, information and story, books and technology (DeCandido, 1999, p. 46).

Advertisements, both print and televised, have often employed images of and references to librarians. Some examples are:

- ▶ Kellogg's Corn Flakes commercial has a prudish librarian "shushing" the rooster.
- ▶ Saturn car commercial with the middle-aged female librarian with glasses, emphasizing quiet in the library. Viewers are supposed to connect it with the quiet ride of the Saturn.
- ▶ A Clairol Herbal Essence commercial set in a library, with a young librarian, hair in a bun, shushing someone. In come the Herbal Essence men, who start washing her hair in the library. In the end she's shaking her long hair all over.
- ▶ A new Honda Accord ad with the quote, "The automotive equivalent of a really hot librarian."

The Internet has given rise to some amusing Web sites in response to media stereotyping which serve both to entertain and offer debunking strategies. The Lipstick Librarian is one of the coolest librarians on the Web. The author (Absher, 2003) describes what makes a "Lipstick Librarian" as: "Money? Fame? Beauty? A mastery of AACR2 and reference interview techniques? No! It's the ability to look fabulous while poking around a dot-matrix printer with a bent paper-clip." At the Web site one can take a quiz to determine if you are a Lipstick Librarian, learn beauty tips such as using the rag-paper/lint stuffing from interlibrary loan envelopes for a mud-pack, and tap into an essential bibliography with resources like: "The Glasses/Earring Ratio: Which Should be Larger?: Accessorizing Library Staff"(Absher, 2002).

Libraristic Links: Librarians on Parade (Smith, 2003) directs one to the Web sites of The Bellydancing Librarian, The Leather Librarian, The Bodybuilding Librarian, Gothique Librarian, and The Modified

Librarian (librarians with tattoos and piercings) among many others. The wide variety of what might be thought of as nontraditional interests and backgrounds of these librarians discredit the stereotype and provide forums for them to interact and have fun.

■ Perpetuating the Stereotype

What about the perception that the stereotype is the reality? In all probability there are students contemplating library studies who believe the school library media center to be a quiet haven where they can retreat from the public. The Internet newsgroup, <alt.support.shyness> recently aired a dialogue between two girls—one working a summer job in a library and the other, a library school student. The girl working the summer job expressed how she was starting to understand where the "shy librarian" stereotype came from and how library work is a great shy job. The library school student, admitting that the profession of librarianship is much more diverse than the stereotype and requires quite a bit of public contact, still encouraged the worker to enter the field and find her niche as an introvert.

Working in a school library media center, not exactly a quiet refuge, can find the school library media specialist multi-tasking the following activities during a typical period:

- ▶ Monitoring students who are finishing homework, reading books, magazines, and newspapers, surfing the Internet, and accessing online databases;
- ▶ Finding a video for a teacher;
- ▶ Answering questions;
- ▶ Recommending a book for a book report;
- ▶ Assisting teachers as they sign up for lessons;
- ▶ Helping students design a multimedia presentation;
- ▶ Working on a book order; and
- ▶ Preparing an in-service program.

Librarianship is a second career choice for many. The largest percentage of students in master's programs in library and information science is in the 45–49 age group (Saye & Wisser, 2001). Why are these people changing careers? Is it failure at their first career choice? What is drawing them to the library profession? School librarianship may also be a "second librarianship" career in that librarians in public or special libraries choose to transition to a school library setting once they become parents, as the school library schedule more closely meshes with that of their children. It is important that when making a transfer from another type of library that the focus shift is from primarily an administrative function to an educational one.

■ Education and Image

The unfortunate image of the school library media specialist could also be a consequence of education. A large number of people serving as school librarians do not have adequate education and a full understanding of how to manage a highly functional school library media program. (This issue is discussed further in the chapter on "Becoming a School Library Media Specialist.") Blanche Woolls (1999) in her President's Message to the International Association of School Librarianship makes this argument:

> School librarians are frequently asked, "Do you have to go to school to be a school librarian?" We feel angry with the person who asks and when we respond, we must sound angry and defensive. Our degree of anger escalates with the years of preparation required of us before we became school librarians, and that may be very different from country to country and from location to location within countries.
>
> The extent of preparation of school librarians ranges from none at all to master's degrees. School librarians are "trained" in workshops given by government agencies, by other school librarians, and in colleges and universities with formal multi-year programs. Sometimes a teaching credential is required before taking school library courses; sometimes certification is granted with no teaching experience. Often persons working in school libraries are, at best, clerks. However we are prepared to manage school libraries, it is how we are perceived, our image, that matters. Why do others find it difficult to recognize the level of effort it takes to become and remain an effective school librarian?
>
> This raises a philosophical question similar to "Which came first, the chicken or the egg?" "Which came first, librarians appointed without training or the image that no one needed any training to be a school librarian?" School libraries began,

at least in the United States, as a stack of books on the corner of the schoolmaster's desk. Early school libraries in separate rooms remained small collections of books under the supervision of a teacher for an hour or so a day. This teacher might have had little, if any, formal training because little, if any, was available.

The image was not positive. The only task perceived as more onerous was management of the study hall, and sometimes, the library shelves were found at the back of the study hall. School librarians always said "Shhhhhh!"

So, the debate between, was the image poor because librarians weren't trained, or were teachers reluctant to choose to become librarians because the image was poor? It is easy to find administrators who believe that almost anyone can run a school library (Woolls, 1999).

■ The Invisible School Librarian

Administrators' indifference to school library media programs and school library media specialists can be traced to a lack of understanding of their value and educational potential, according to Gary Hartzell, a former principal and current educational administration professor. Hartzell wrote a compelling piece, "The Invisible School Librarian: Why Other Educators Are Blind to Your Value" (1997) in which he declared, "Mostly, it's just a matter of indifference—and people regard as expendable those things about which they are indifferent" (p. 25).

The reasons administrators are indifferent, maintains Hartzell, stem from their teacher training, the kind of work librarians do, and traditional school librarian culture. Most administrators receive little or no training about the role of the library. There is no mention of library programs in their textbooks or within their curriculum. Administrators may only study the library in law classes where it is treated as a source of problems from censorship to copyright. The work librarians do is perceived as one step removed from students and it's hard to measure the extent and quality of their contribution. The school librarian is isolated and there is usually only one per school so there is no strength in numbers. Finally, Hartzell maintains that school librarians may be overlooked because school librarians have done a poor job of promoting themselves. "Influence derives from others' perceptions of what someone can do for them, with them, or to them. Without that perception in place, it is impossible for anyone to influence others. Librarians have generally not done their homework in shaping perceptions in either the field of education or at the district and building level" (p. 26).

There are three strategies that can be used to improve the status of librarians and libraries, Hartzell explains. First is to consciously strive to build influence with the administration and powerful teachers in your school and district. Second is to write articles and make presentations for educators other than librarians. The third is to become active in state and national school library associations.

Many of the solutions put forth by Hartzell fall into the realm of good public relations. Good public relations strategies can assist school librarians in improving their status. Dee Parks (2001), a 35-year school library media specialist, uses a plethora of tactics to interest students and promote good will among faculty and students. She explains, "Neither the best equipment nor the most beautiful facilities will attract patrons if the librarian is not a "people" person who makes customers feel welcome and treats their requests as important. It takes a concentrated effort on the librarian's part to become part of the school. Neither faculty nor students should ever hesitate to ask the librarian for anything they need" (p. 24).

The following is a list of some of Parks' positive approaches:

- help teachers and seniors find materials for college classes they are taking;
- send birthday cards to every teacher;
- videotape in the classroom for those "afraid of the camera;"
- coordinate prom;
- make special trips to pick up books that teachers or students wanted quickly; and
- encourage classes to display their work in the library.

The image that administrators, teachers, and the public perceive about school library media specialists starts with individuals they know personally in the field. It is the professional duty of each school library media specialist to debunk negative librarian stereotypes. A variety of tools and resources exist for public relations ideas for school library media centers, which, if used effectively, can promote positive images of the school library media specialist and library media program.

Questions for Discussion and Reflection

1. Relate your experiences of instances where you have encountered stereotypes of librarians portrayed in the movies, on television, in advertising, or through personal encounters.

2. What can you do on an individual level to debunk stereotypes of librarians?

3. Identify some groups of people who may have misperceptions about school library media specialists. Define these misperceptions and develop solutions to correct them.

4. How might the school library media program suffer because of stereotypes of librarians?

5. How has certification and educational requirements for school library media specialists affected their image in your state?

Projects

1. Do a literature search of newspaper articles and news show transcripts on school librarians/school library media specialists that have been mentioned in the news in your state in the past few years. Report on instances where the librarian stereotype has been referenced.

2. Rent the video of *Desk Set* and compare and contrast its plot to what is happening today with computers in the library and librarians.

3. Create a public relations campaign to elevate the image of school librarians in your state.

References

Absher, L. (2001, October 1). *What is a Lipstick Librarian?* In Lipstick Librarian. Retrieved September 17, 2002, from <www.lipsticklibrarian.com/whatis.html>.

DeCandido, G.A. (1999, September). Bibliographic good vs. evil in *Buffy the Vampire Slayer. American Libraries, 30* (8), 44–47.

Hartzell, G. (1997, November). The invisible school librarian: Why other educators are blind to your value. *School Library Journal, 43* (11), 25–29.

The Internet Public Library. (n.d.). *Image of librarians' resources.* Retrieved July 7, 2003, from University of Michigan, School of Information, The Regents of the University of Michigan Web site at: <www.ipl.org/ref/RR/static/hum45.10.50.html>.

Marinelli, S., & Baker, T. (2003). Media images. In *Stereotypes of Librarians.* Retrieved July 7, 2003, from <home.earthlink.net/~cyberresearcher/stereotypes.htm>.

Parks, D. (2001, Sept/Oct). The enduring power of PR. *The Book Report, 20* (2), 24.

Raish, M. (2002). *Librarians in the movies: An annotated filmography.* Retrieved July 7, 2003, from <www.byui.edu/Ricks/employee/raishm/films/introduction.html>.

Saye, J.D., & Wisser, K.M. (2001). Students. In *Library and information science education statistical report 2001.* Retrieved September 17, 2002, from <ils.unc.edu/ALISE/2001/Students/Students01.htm>.

Smith, B. (2003). Libraristic links. In *Libraristic.com.* Retrieved July 7, 2003, from <www.librarism.com/parade.html>.

Stevens, N. (1988, Spring). Our image in the 1980s. *Library Trends, 36* (4), 825–851.

Woolls, B. (1999, June). Preparing school librarians—An image problem? [Electronic version]. *IASL Newsletter.* Retrieved July 7, 2003, from <www.iasl-slo.org/presjune99.html>.

Additional Information

Barron, D.D., & Knapp, E. (2001, October). The library media specialist and the first-year teacher: A partnership revisited. *School Library Media Activities Monthly, 18* (2), 49–51.

Flowers, H.F. (1998). *Public relations for the school library: 500 ways to influence people and win friends for your school library media center.* New York: Neal-Schuman.

Hartzell, G.N. (2000, March/April). Being proactive. *The Book Report, 20* (2), 14–19.

Hartzell, G.N. (1994). *Building influence for the school librarian.* Worthington, OH: Linworth Publishing.

Howe, E.B. (2001, January/February) Ten tips for leadership. *Knowledge Quest, 29* (2), 16–19.

McElmeel, S.L. (Ed.). (2000) *Tips: Ideas for secondary school librarians and technology specialists* (2nd ed.). Worthington, OH: Linworth Publishing.

Snyder, T.D. (2000). *Getting lead-bottomed administrators excited about school library media centers.* Littleton, CO: Libraries Unlimited.

Valenza, J.K. (1998). *Power tools: 100+ essential forms and presentations for your school library media program.* Chicago: American Library Association.

Web Sites

Librarian Avengers
<www.librarianavengers.org>
A humorous site developed by a graduate library school student about public perceptions, quirks of the job, and more. Includes a diary of her journey toward getting her degree.

NewBreed Librarian
<www.newbreedlibrarian.org>
This online bimonthly publication intends to foster a sense of community for those new to librarianship, whether in school or

recently graduated. It features interviews and highlights progressive librarians and other information professionals.

You Don't Look Like a Librarian!: Librarians' views of public perception in the Internet age
<atst.nso.edu/library/perception>
Results of a survey of librarians about librarians and their image. An extensive bibliography includes stories of librarians in the news and links to "sites with attitude."

DIVERGENT PERSPECTIVES

Staffing the School Library Media Center

Of all the variables that affect a school library media program, staffing is the most critical. A well-trained, professional, school library media specialist can work to creatively overcome barriers of poor facilities and limited budgets. A full-time school library media specialist in an elementary school is capable of instilling the love of reading in students and working collaboratively with teachers to enhance lessons. Resources, selected by a professional, will support the curriculum and provide a school with more value for its dollar. Conversely, a state-of-the-art facility can sit idle while one overworked school library media specialist bounces between several schools or troubleshoots technology. A clerk running a school library media center may see to it that books are circulated and shelved, but does not have the training to sustain a vision of a program or create a foundation for lifelong learning.

Perhaps nowhere is the case made more convincingly for employing professional staff in school library media centers than in the research of Keith Curry Lance (2000) and his colleagues. Their evidence has been established in the following settings:

▶ The Alaska study demonstrated the importance of a full-time library media specialist who is involved in instructional activities. In elementary schools with a well-developed library media program, 86% of the students scored proficient or above on state reading tests, compared with 73%t of the students in schools with less developed library media programs.

- ▶ In Pennsylvania, the success of the school library media program in promoting high academic achievement was dependent on adequate staffing on all three grade levels tested. Adequate staffing was defined as at least one full-time certified library media specialist and one full-time support member.
- ▶ In Colorado, students' reading scores correlated with the involvement of the library media specialist in instructional and leadership activities and the number of professional librarians.

The American Association of School Librarians' (AASL) in their "Position Statement on Appropriate Staffing for School Library Media Centers" recommends:

- ▶ The success of any school library media program, no matter how well designed, depends ultimately on the quality and number of the personnel responsible for the program. A well-educated and highly motivated professional staff, adequately supported by technical and clerical staff, is critical to the endeavor.
- ▶ Although staffing patterns are developed to meet local needs, certain basic staffing requirements can be identified. Staffing patterns must reflect the following principles:
  - All students, teachers, and administrators in each school building at all grade levels must have access to a library media program provided by one or more certificated library media specialist working full-time in the school's library media center.
  - Both professional personnel and support staff are necessary for all library media programs at all grade levels. Each school must employ at least one full-time technical assistant or clerk for each library media specialist. Some programs, facilities, and levels of service will require more than one support staff member for each professional.
  - More than one library media professional is required in many schools. The specific number of additional professional staff is determined by the school's size, number of

students and number of teachers, facilities, specific library program. A reasonable ratio of professional staff to teacher and student populations is required in order to provide for the levels of service and library media program development described in *Information Power: Guidelines For School Library Media Programs*.

All school systems must employ a district library media director to provide leadership and direction to the overall library media program. The district director is a member of the administrative staff and serves on committees that determine the criteria and policies for the district's curriculum and instructional programs. The director communicates the goals and needs of both the school and district library media programs to the superintendent, board of education, other district-level personnel, and the community. In this advocacy role, the district library media director advances the concept of the school library media specialist as a partner with teachers and promotes a staffing level that allows the partnership to flourish (AASL, 1991).

Divergent Perspectives

If professional staff can make such a difference, why do divergent perspectives surrounding staffing of school library media centers exist? Part of the issue can be traced to state staffing mandates which run the spectrum from schools being directed to employ one or more certified school library media specialists in all schools to utilizing anyone with a high school diploma to run a school library (Everhart, 2002). Misunderstandings of the role of the school librarian by the administration can lead to unsatisfactory staffing practices when stringent mandates aren't in place. The flood of technology into the school library media center has staffing ramifications in the areas of added duties and cooperation with technology coordinators and computer teachers.

■ Staffing Mandates

Although all states have certification requirements in place for school library media specialists, having a certified person employed in every school library within that state is not a certainty. If it sounds like a contradiction, it is. Of the 50 states and the District of Columbia, only 20, or less than half, have a mandate for employing certified staff in the school library media center. A listing of all the states, mandates, and ratio of students per school library media specialist appears in Figure 1 on pp. 43–44. Obviously, states with mandates for school library media specialists employ more of them.

When states without mandates utilize site-based management, school library media specialists can be victims. In a site-based managed school, it is the principal, or perhaps a team composed of the principal, faculty, and community members, which make decisions as to how to spend money. Therefore, when budgets are tight, it is often the school library media specialist that is let go as the following scenarios illustrate:

1. In Kalamazoo, Michigan, 11 of 18 elementary school librarians were cut in response to a school district budget shortfall. What hurt the elementary librarians was that they worked part-time, leaving them little time to develop their programs (Glick, 2000).
2. Elementary librarians in Rochester, Minnesota, must now shuttle between three media centers instead of two and the media services coordinator position has been cut (Glick, 2001).
3. Few California elementary schools have certified librarians. And while many districts have certified people in secondary schools, it is just as common to find districts without a single library professional (Glick, 2000).

Doug Johnson (2002), a frequent author and presenter in the field, regards the cutting of professional and clerical staff a crisis. "Let's just face it, good school library media programs may never be seen as a permanent part of the educational landscape. Gifted and talented programs, art programs, academic and athletic extra-curricular programs, and even school counseling programs—anything in a school that goes beyond one teacher, 30 students and a textbook—can and will be seen as non-essential by some decision-makers. I am not sure that this is a bad thing. Our very vulnerability demands that we as a profession need to continually find ways to strengthen our programs and roles. I would suggest we take a hard look at the challenges we currently face and see how we can rise to meet them" (Johnson, 2002, p. 21).

■ Shortage of School Library Media Specialists

The fragile state of job security and lack of support for the position discourages people from going into school librarianship. This, combined with a surge in retirements, has resulted in a nationwide shortage of school library media specialists.

Research in state staffing practices has revealed the following:

- ▶ Mississippi and Oklahoma added staffing mandates in the 90s, but there weren't enough candidates to fill the mandated positions (Everhart, 1998; 2000).
- ▶ Pennsylvania dropped its state mandate for school librarians in 1993. Although the aftermath of dropping the mandate was not felt immediately, the effects became apparent as school librarians began retiring. School librarian spots are being left vacant—especially when it is so difficult to find candidates. If a position lies dormant for an extended period of time, it can be convenient for a principal to just stop trying and phase out the job (Everhart, 2000).
- ▶ Forty-six states reported severe or extremely severe shortages of school library media specialists (Everhart, 2002).
- ▶ In Kentucky, gaining a state mandate in 2000 for library media specialists was a double-edged sword—many schools were surprised that having a school librarian wasn't a requirement. Many schools also didn't know that hiring part-time media specialists was an option and began exercising that right (Everhart, 2002).

To compensate for shortages, teachers are hired to staff those school libraries while simultaneously working on their certification. How does this reflect on the profession? How can someone with minimal training administer a multifaceted program like those described in *Information Power*? Which teachers are volunteering to staff the media center? Is it the dynamic and creative ones who see the library as an avenue to interact with more students and spread their wings or are they teachers who perceive the school library media center to be an easy avenue to escape the classroom?

■ Paraprofessionals

A teacher working on certification while simultaneously running a school library is actually a better state of affairs than what occurs in some schools with site-based management and no mandates for professional staffing. Often, especially in elementary schools, paraprofessional aides will be in charge of the school library. They sometimes seek help from professional librarians on LM_NET, leading to heated discussions. Over 60 participants posted messages with the heading "Uneducated Librarians," debating the topic with conflicting views such as:

- ▶ Acknowledgement by school library media specialists that paraprofessionals can do a good job of running a media center, but are having problems when they are in charge of teaching. This breeds resentment from professional school library media specialists who describe a double standard when paraprofessionals are not allowed to teach in other subject areas in schools, such as science and math.
- ▶ Paraprofessionals taking exception to being labeled "uneducated," because they have attended workshops and professional meetings in order to help faculty and students. Many feel that some professional school library media specialists do poor jobs, regardless of degrees acquired, and some paraprofessionals have turned lackluster programs into dynamic ones.
- ▶ School library media specialists who have trained aides for several years and later find them overstepping their bounds by attempting to take on professional duties. Some professionals have trained aides only to find their own position eliminated and duties given to the same aide.
- ▶ School library media specialists and paraprofessionals who believe that aides are being exploited by schools that hire them to do the work of a professional and pay them the salary of a clerk.

■ Staffing and Technology

The influx of technology into schools has expanded the responsibilities of the school library media specialist. Three out of four school librarians recommend or evaluate vendors for online references, databases, and library computer software, with nearly half doing so when it comes to library computer hardware and the Internet (Lau, 2002). Some even assist in the selection of computer software and CDs for the classroom. When it comes to the school's technology coordinator, 68% of librarians say the relationship is truly collaborative, with nearly half sharing the technology-related buying decisions (Lau, 2002).

Technology coordinators come with a variety of qualifications. This could potentially influence their relationship with the school library media specialist, even resulting in turf wars. For example, some tech coordinators are hired for their high levels of technical skills — setting up and maintaining networks, troubleshooting hardware, and installing software. They don't have the background of integrating technology into the curriculum, support for teaching, staff development, and knowledge of educational resources. But they may be given authority in those areas with the librarian in a subordinate position. Other tech coordinators are teachers with a supplemental degree in such areas as computer education, educational technology, or educational media. Clashes may occur in the division of teaching roles with the school library media specialist.

It is important to define roles and responsibilities between the school library media specialist and tech coordinator. Areas where conflict may arise are:

- ▶ creation of the library's Web page;
- ▶ teaching responsibilities for electronic resources;
- ▶ software purchasing;
- ▶ decision making about the school's network;
- ▶ long-range planning for technology;
- ▶ privacy and safety; and
- ▶ policies concerning the library's computers.

For those schools without technology coordinators, districts often try to control their soaring technology support costs by using library media specialists. Some library media specialists have found they now have two jobs instead of one. Their extra layer of responsibilities include: keeping networks functioning; making printers behave; maintaining detailed records on malfunctions; negotiating with vendors; teaching software applications; writing grant applications; and attending professional development in technology. This strategy "does not really save money; it simply transfers the cost to teacher [or librarian] salaries.

What's more, relying on teachers and other non-technical staff could have an impact on their productivity" (Fitzgerald, 2002).

It is common sense that when school librarians are shouldering the burden for school or district-wide technology support, the library program will suffer. These duties are exceptionally time-consuming. School library media specialists who were drawn to the field because of a love of books and working with children, may find little time to do the things they are good at and enjoy in their library role. Administrators rely on the wording in many teaching contracts, "and other duties as assigned," to justify the added responsibilities.

On the other hand, some regard the marriage between their librarian and technology coordinator roles to be natural and beneficial. People in their buildings look to them as the source of information in all formats. The school library media center has realized the status as the "hub of the school" that is so often heralded. School library media specialists have more visibility and recognition as team players. Several receive higher pay in the form of bonuses, overtime, or by elevation to an administrative salary scale. Fixed scheduling may get switched to flexible scheduling to allow time for both roles. School library media specialists who commuted between several schools are assigned to just one when they take on technology. Others, in states without mandates, believe that taking the responsibility for technology has given them job security.

Staffing patterns and related job responsibilities in school library media centers vary widely throughout the United States. The method a school district uses to staff its school library media centers is usually indicative of the level of importance it places on school library media programs.

Figure 1: State Mandates for School Library Media Specialists with Ratios of Students Per School Library Media Specialist (Everhart, 2002).

STATE	STUDENTS PER SLMS	STATE MANDATE	MANDATE IS
North Dakota	312	NO	
Arkansas	437	YES	FT in all schools over 300 students
Oregon	451	YES	One FT per district
Vermont	455	YES	FT in all schools over 300 students
Kansas	458	YES	FT in all schools
Montana	466	YES	FT in all schools over 251 students
Nebraska	511	YES	FT in all schools over 750 students
Kentucky	521	YES	FT in all schools
Rhode Island	522	YES	FT in all HS
Alabama	549	NO	
District of Columbia	551	NO	
Missouri	559	YES	FT in all schools over 800 students
North Carolina	569	NO	
South Carolina	576	YES	FT in MS & HS over 400; E over 375
Oklahoma	636	YES	FT in all schools over 500 students
Tennessee	645	YES	FT in K–8 over 550; HS over 300 students
South Dakota	658	NO	
Iowa	659	NO	
Wisconsin	661	YES	FT in all HS and MS; E under supervision of certified SLMS
Hawaii	670	YES	FT in all schools
New Jersey	672	NO	
Louisiana	680	NO	
Mississippi	689	YES	FT in all schools over 500 students
New Hampshire	701	NO	

STATE	STUDENTS PER SLMS	STATE MANDATE	MANDATE IS
Georgia	733	YES	FT in all schools over 251 students
Maine	733	NO	
Washington	741	NO	
Wyoming	772	NO	
Texas	773	NO	
Virginia	782	YES	FT in all schools over 300 students
Colorado	800	NO	
Pennsylvania	825	NO	
Minnesota	833	NO	
West Virginia	852	NO	
New York	860	YES	One FT in grades 7–12 per 1,000 students
Maryland	863	YES	FT in all schools over 200 students
Florida	869	NO	
Connecticut	955	NO	
Indiana	1,006	NO	
Arizona	1,009	NO	
Michigan	1,052	NO	
Illinois	1,052	YES	FT in all HS
Delaware	1,052	NO	
Ohio	1,107	NO	
Nevada	1,157	NO	
New Mexico	1,220	NO	
Alaska	1,268	NO	
Idaho	1,310	NO	
Massachusetts	1,498	NO	
Utah	1,650	NO	
California	4,363	NO	

Questions for Discussion and Reflection

1. Debate the pros and cons of experience vs. education for the position of school library media specialist.

2. What might be reasons why some states have mandates for school library media specialists and others don't? Why would a state change from having a mandate to not having one, or vice versa?

3. What types of interview questions would you ask a library clerk candidate? A technology coordinator?

4. What is the mandate for school library media staffing in your state? How does it affect how school libraries are staffed in your area?

5. Discuss some strategies you might use to prevent your school administrator from assigning you responsibilities for school-wide technology.

Projects

1. Choose a local school and analyze the instructional program requirements, number of students and teachers served, and other pertinent features of the school and the program to determine appropriate staffing patterns. Prepare an advocacy plan for appropriate numbers of professional and other staff to meet the learning needs of the school's learning community.

2. Visit a school library media center and observe the staff's activities. Compare what you witness to the issues discussed in this chapter.

3. Use the resources at the Library Research Service Web site to prepare a presentation that could be given to a school board on the impact of professional school library media staffing on student achievement. Simulate the scenario that professional staff is about to be cut in your district.

References

American Association of School Librarians. (1991). *Position statement on appropriate staffing for school library media center*. Retrieved July 7, 2003, from <www.ala.org/aasl/positions/ps_schoolmedia.html>.

Everhart, N. (1998, August). The prognosis, doctor? *School Library Journal, 44* (8), 32–35.

Everhart, N. (2000, September). Looking for a few good librarians. *School Library Journal, 46* (9), 58–61.

Everhart, N. (2002, June). Filling the void. *School Library Journal 48* (6), 44–49.

Fitzgerald, S. (2002). Technology's true cost [Electronic version]. *American School Board Journal*. Retrieved July 7, 2003, from American School Board Journal Web site at <www.asbj.com/schoolspending/fitzgerald.html>.

Glick, A. (2000, February). California dreamin. *School Library Journal, 46* (2), 16–17.

Glick, A. (2000, July). Canned in Kalamazoo under pressure to shave costs, 11 schools vote to eliminate their librarians. *School Library Journal, 46* (7), 14–15.

Glick, A. (2001, June). Budget ax falls on Minnesota schools. *School Library Journal 47* (6), 18.

Johnson, D. (2002, May/June). The seven most critical challenges that face our profession. *Teacher Librarian, 29* (5), 21–23.

Lance, K.C., Hamilton-Pennell, C., Rodney, M.J., & Hainer, E. (2000, April). Dick and Jane go to the head of the class. *School Library Journal, 46* (4), 44–47.

Lau, D. (2002, May). Got clout? *School Library Journal, 48* (5), 40–45.

Additional Information

Johnson, D. Librarians are from Venus; technicians are from Mars. *Technology Connection, 5* (3), 48.

Torres, N. (2001, November/December). When librarians become computer technicians. *Library Talk, 14* (5), 32–33.

Web Sites

AASL Affiliate Assembly Directory of State and Regional Affiliate Organizations
<www.ala.org/aasl/aa_directory.html>
This directory links to each state's professional school library media organization where updates on staffing issues may be posted.

Library Research Service School Library Media Impact Studies
<www.lrs.org/html/about/school_studies.html>
Provides sample reports from studies conducted in Colorado, Pennsylvania, and Alaska, and related news stories.

Roles for Education Paraprofessionals in Effective Schools
<www.ed.gov/pubs/Paraprofessionals>
A 1997 report from the U.S. Department of Education that describes roles, supplies job descriptions, and profiles effective programs.

Schools and Staffing Survey, 1999–2000: Overview of the Data for Public, Private, Public Charter, and Bureau of Indian Affairs Elementary and Secondary Schools
<nces.ed.gov/pubsearch/pubsinfo.asp?pubid=2002313>
Information on school library media center staffing patterns is provided in this federal report.

Standards and Guidelines

How many tables and chairs should I have? How many books? What types of information literacy skills should students be learning? What is an appropriate budget for my school library media center's size? In a neighboring district the elementary school library media center has a clerk and I don't, even though they have a smaller library than me. Why don't I have one? As a new school library media specialist, you may find yourself asking some of these questions. Many of the answers can be located in local, state, and national standards (sometimes referred to as guidelines) for school library media programs.

Not all 50 states have standards for school library media programs, but many do. In most instances, the state department of education develops these standards. The "State Pages Relating to School Library/Media Services" (Bertland, 2003) Web site is a comprehensive starting point that links to school library media information in state departments of education. Often, one can find the full-text of any applicable standards at these state sites. If not, there may be contact information where you can inquire about a state's school library media standards. Occasionally, guidelines are created by professional organizations within a state—especially if there is a lack of school library media leadership in the state department of education. The Web site, "Directory of State and Regional Affiliate Organizations" of the American Association of School Librarians (2003) is a similar source for professional organization sites. In a number of cases, the department of education and state professional organization work as a team to develop standards. Larger school districts might also have created their own local standards for school library media programs. The national guidelines, *Information Power: Building Partnerships for Learning*, were published by the American Association of School Librarians and the Association for Educational Communications and Technology in 1998.

Standards vary as to their content, depth, and approach. *Information Power* is broad-based and philosophical. Its standards are qualitative—no baseline numerical recommendations are specified for such things as collection size, budget, number of personnel, numbers of computers, or dimensions of the facility. For example, *Information Power* recommends that the "collections of the library media program are developed and evaluated collaboratively to support the school's curriculum and to meet the diverse learning needs of students" (AASL/AECT, p. 90). State and local standards tend to be more of a quantitative nature—precise numbers, or quantities, are specified for collection size, budget, number of personnel, numbers of computers, or dimensions of the facility. In Massachusetts (Professional Standards Committee of the Massachusetts School Library Media Association, 1997), the standard size for school library media collections is:

- ▶ Less than 400 students—20 print titles per student
- ▶ 401–800 students—22 print titles per student
- ▶ More than 801 students—24 print titles per student
- ▶ Seventy percent of the entire print collection must have a copyright date no later than ten years from the current year.

As a general rule, library standards and guidelines are not laws requiring enforcement, but are recommendations. There are school library state laws, which have been legislated, and education department regulations, which are legally enforceable. Most laws and regulations are quantitative and, therefore, deal with staffing and certification. However, some may deal with programming. New York State is a case in point. Education department regulations require each secondary school library media center to employ a full-time certified school library media specialist. No such requirement exists for elementary schools. New York also has legislated over the years that each school receives six dollars per student for library resources. On the other hand, the New York State Education Department has developed a rubric, which evaluates school library media programs in 15 distinct areas both quantitatively and qualitatively (Roscello, 2000). This document can only serve as a guide, and school library media programs are not obligated to implement it. Texas has also developed comprehensive guidelines for school library media programs, but its legislative mandate states only: "A school district shall consider the standards in developing, implementing, or expanding library services" (Texas State Library & Archives Commission, 2003).

The issue of standards, guidelines, regulations, and mandates is confusing. Even veteran school library media specialists, under false impressions at times, believe that a guideline is a mandate when it isn't. That is why it is important to join and stay active in your state professional school library media organization where members are updated regularly on these concerns.

Divergent Perspectives

Discussion about standards has focused on the best types of standards, their enforceability, their communication to the right people, and how well they reflect the reality of school library media programs.

■ Qualitative vs. Quantitative Standards

What types of standards are most useful—qualitative or quantitative? Proponents of quantitative standards maintain that there is no arguing with numbers. They are straightforward and simple to use for evaluation and comparison purposes. You can easily determine whether or not you have reached quantitative goals. Numbers can be used to alert and convince administrators. They are particularly useful to new school library media specialists and when planning or managing a brand new school library. It is good to have baseline figures for collections, facility size, equipment, and furnishings to get started.

Administrators can place too much emphasis on counting things to meet requirements with little regard to their quality (Woolls, 1999). Poor collections and equipment could be left gathering dust so as to meet an arbitrary numerical score. "Administrators may also buy inferior products to achieve a standard number of holdings rather than purchase high-quality merchandise" (Woolls, 1999, p. 235). So, in order to meet a standard of ten books per student, you could end up having a dated, shoddy collection.

As more school library media centers incorporate electronic resources, quantitative collection guidelines will have little significance.

Determining if students are successfully integrating these resources into their schoolwork becomes more important. The physical size of the library media center will have less meaning also as students will be able to access these resources from virtually any location. School library media specialists will have to rely on qualitative guidelines, like the Information Literacy Standards for Student Learning found in *Information Power*, to assist them in virtual school library environments.

Qualitative program regulations are difficult to enforce due to interpretation. A typical qualitative program guideline might call for the school library media facility to contain areas for large and small groups and individuals. A quantitative program guideline might say that there should be room in the facility to seat 10% of the student population or two classes. A budget figure of twenty dollars per student cannot be disputed as can one that "supports the objectives of the library program."

A compromise approach is that of good, better, best. Rather than meet a one-dimensional standard, other states, like previously mentioned New York and Texas, have developed rubrics that measure graduated levels of quality. Perhaps in response to school library media specialists desiring some quantitative standards related to *Information Power*, a national rubric (AASL Teaching for Learning Task Force Assessment Rubric Subcommittee, 1999) was designed to assess school library media programs. This tool is a set of criteria that tells you if your media center is at the basic, proficient, or exemplary level in several categories by describing scenarios at each level. It is envisioned that school library media specialists going over the documents with their administrators will make necessary program changes.

■ Authority of Standards

To some, it doesn't really matter if standards are qualitative or quantitative if they are simply guidelines that have no authority. "As long as the standards are voluntary, and my school board is told it doesn't have to do it, it's not going to happen," is the lament of many school library media specialists. Comments like this were offered at public hearings when Texas was developing its new standards (Olson & Glick, 1997).

Probably the biggest issue with standards is that voluntary standards are not enforceable, so few schools will meet them. Research on staffing mandates in individual states backs up this claim (Everhart, 1998). Those states with the most stringent mandates for certified staff had the lowest student per school library media specialist ratios because they were forced to by regulations. If you can't get a school to hire a certified staff member, can you expect it to implement flexible scheduling voluntarily?

There have been some creative methods used to bolster voluntary standards with authority. Minnesota's Educational Media Organization solicited endorsements of support from school board associations, curriculum associations, reading associations, teacher organizations, and administrative associations for its state standards. It also developed a checklist for parents to help them determine the status of their own children's media programs (Johnson, 2000). Texas is trying to get grass roots support for its standards by publishing the names of schools with exemplary libraries in the newspapers and announcing them on TV. Parental pressure as to why their child's school library media center isn't on the list may work to support the standards (Olson & Glick, 1997).

There is recourse if a school is violating mandates for the school library media program or other areas. Some states have hotlines whereby you can contact education departments anonymously and report infractions. An investigator determines if a school is violating laws or regulations. If it is, the school will be directed to improve the situation and may even face losing state funding.

■ Communicating Standards

Does anyone outside the school library media profession even know that standards exist for school library media programs? Standards are often developed by school library media specialists in isolation and without input from teachers or administrators. Standards can be peppered with professional jargon that makes them hard to understand outside of a limited circle.

Gary Hartzell, a writer who frequently explores the relationship between library media specialists and administrators, notes that administrators don't care about standards for school media programs because they have never been taught to care. "To make a difference in real schools, the AASL needs first to come up with ways to make the people who decide budgets, jobs, staffing, scheduling, curriculum, evaluation, etc. want to read the book and think seriously about its recommendations. Unless new library roles and standards are recognized, adopted, and supported by boards, administrators, and teachers, they will have no value in strengthening libraries, library programs, or librarians in the schools" (Hartzell, 1995). He feels our needs must be communicated to administrators in their journals and at their conferences.

Some organizations create materials that school library media specialists can use to publicize and promote standards to various groups. Aids such as brochures (AASL, 2003) and PowerPoint™ presentations (Roscello, 2000) are ready-made communication tools that work to sway administrators, legislators, and parents to support school library media programs. School library media specialists need to use these tools proactively.

Another source for communicating standards lies in *Information Power* itself. For each of the Information Literacy Standards, scenarios called "Standards in Action" describe how the standards apply in various subject areas and settings. One example is:

> Grades 9–12 (English Language Arts) Students need to identify a person living today who meets a literary definition of a tragic hero and to find information to support their choices. As a class, students develop a rubric to identify the essential traits of a tragic hero and to specify the kind and amount of evidence to "certify" someone as a contemporary tragic hero. After using biographical information to begin a list of potential tragic heroes, students explore a wide range of other resources to amass as much authoritative evidence as possible to support their choices. The class judges each case against the rubric (AASL/AECT, pp. 16–17).

These scenarios, practical and useful when presenting standards information, can be adapted to your own situation. In the case in point above, "folk hero" might possibly be substituted for the literary definition, the grade level reduced to third grade, and books of tall tales replace biographical reference sources. Thus, the same standard is addressed at a lower level. In order to raise your principal's awareness that you are addressing national (or state) standards, clearly note on your lesson plans or in your monthly report whenever they are being implemented.

■ Are Standards Realistic?

Information Power contains a vision and guiding principles for school library media programs. "School library media specialists must determine how to interpret these themes and incorporate them into the functions of their individual school media programs. The dynamics of each situation—local policies, personnel, budgets, and communities—and the individual school library media specialist's own style are factors to be considered" (AASL/AECT, 1998, p. 47). Implementing Information Power at the local level may be difficult due to these factors.

Library school dean, Keith Swigger (1999), critically reviewed *Information Power* and evaluated its effectiveness in preparing library school students for the profession. He stated, "Good library education is pragmatic. To get jobs and do good in the world, students must have a realistic grasp of librarianship. They won't get it from reading IP2" (p. 32). Swigger argued that the national standards confuse the roles of school librarianship and teaching and are filled with logical errors and untrue assertions. He is judgmental that IP2 (*Information Power: Building Partnerships for Learning*) confuses student attitudes and values with abilities and skills and that the standards were developed with little input from those outside school librarianship.

Information Power is unique because it is the first set of student-centered national standards that focuses on the impact of the school library media program on learning. Although this may seem abstract at first, it is critical that school library media specialists take this approach with their programs, as schools in general are being held more and more accountable via the standardized test scores of the students.

A plethora of qualitative and quantitative tools exist at the local, state, and national levels to guide and assist school library media specialists. By becoming knowledgeable about these tools, school library media specialists can utilize them to develop outstanding school library media programs.

Questions for Discussion and Reflection

1. What types of program standards might you find the most useful as a new school library media specialist? Why?

2. Discuss ways to draw on information from standards to convince your principal that you need a budget increase for program improvements.

3. Are you aware of any legislative mandates for school library media programs in your state? What is their effect on school library media centers?

4. What changes have occurred since *Information Power* was published in 1998, and what changes might occur in the next five years that you feel should be reflected in the next set of national guidelines?

5. What makes a good school library media center?

Projects

1. Find out if your state has standards for school library media programs. If so, get a copy of the standards and use them to evaluate a local school library media center. Discuss with the school library media specialist how he or she attempts to address the standards and the obstacles he or she encounters along the way.

2. Prepare a PowerPoint™ presentation that you would give to the faculty of your school. The goal of the presentation is to educate the faculty about how you would like to work together to address a particular Learning and Teaching Principle of School Library Media Programs found on page 58 of *Information Power*.

3. Using the Web site, "State Pages Relating to School Library/Media Services," locate and print out the standards for school library media programs from two states. Compare and contrast them.

References

American Association of School Librarians. (2003, July 8). *Directory of state and regional affiliate organizations*. Retrieved July 8, 2003, from <www.ala.org/aasl/aa_directory.html>.

American Association of School Librarians. (2003, July 2). *Principal's manual brochure*. Retrieved July 8, 2002, from <www.ala.org/aasl/principalsmanual.html>.

American Association of School Librarians, & Association for Educational Communications and Technology. (1998). *Information power: Building partnerships for learning*. Chicago: American Library Association.

American Association of School Librarians Teaching for Learning Task Force Assessment Rubric Subcommittee. (1999). School library media program assessment rubric for the 21st century. In Adcock, D.C. (Ed.), *A planning guide for Information Power: Building partnerships for learning* (pp. 29–46). Chicago: American Association of School Librarians.

Bertland, L. (2003). *State pages relating to school library/media services*. Retrieved July 8, 2003, from <www.sldirectory.com/libsf/stlibs.html>.

Everhart, N. (1998, August). The prognosis, doctor? *School Library Journal, 44* (8), 32–35.

Hartzell, G. (1995, December 8). Re: (Fwd) New national guidelines for school. Message posted to <ericir.syr.edu/Virtual/Listserv_Archives/LM_NET-pre1997/1995/Dec_1995/msg00508.html>.

Johnson, D. (2000, December). Building standards that are useful. *Teacher-Librarian, 28* (2), 19–20.

Olson, R., & Glick, A. (1997, May). Books, bytes, & BBQ. *School Library Journal, 43* (5), 31.

Professional standards committee of the Massachusetts School Library Media Association. (1997). *Standards for school library media centers in the Commonwealth of Massachusetts*. Retrieved September 17, 2002, from <www.doe.mass.edu/mailings/1997/lmstandards.html>.

Roscello, F. (2000). *Quality, not quantity.* Retrieved July 8, 2003, from: <www.emsc.nysed.gov/nyc/Library/Documents/N-Rubrics%202000.ppt>.

Swigger, K. (1999, January). Weighing in on IP2. *School Library Journal, 45* (1), 32–37.

Texas State Library & Archives Commission. (n.d.). School library programs: Standards and guidelines for Texas. Retrieved July 8, 2003, from <www.tsl.state.tx.us/ld/schoollibs/standards.html>.

Woolls, B. (1999). The school library media manager (2nd ed.). Englewood, CO: Libraries Unlimited.

Web Sites

American Association of School Librarians
<www.ala.org/aasl>
The official site of the American Association of School Librarians. There is often news of what is happening with standards in the 50 states and nationally.

Library Research Service
<www.lrs.org>
The Library Research Service site that provides results of research studies conducted in school library media centers, statistics, and measurements.

Collection Development

Developing a well-rounded school library media center collection is central to every school library media program. A first-rate collection entices users to the library media center and facilitates learning, which makes the school library media specialist's job easier. If the collection of resources is small, dated, in poor physical condition, uninteresting, and narrow in scope, curriculum support will be limited to encouraging students to read. Today's school library media center collections also consist of electronic resources that require the same attention to development as traditional print ones.

There are many procedures associated with developing and maintaining a school library media center collection (Van Orden & Bishop, 2001):

1. Becoming knowledgeable about an existing collection or creating one;
2. Becoming familiar with the community (that is, the external environment);
3. Assessing the needs of the school's curriculum and other programs as well as the needs of users;
4. Establishing collection development policies and procedures (the overall plan);
5. Creating the basis for selection (including policies and procedures to guide selection decisions);
6. Identifying criteria for evaluating materials;

7. Planning for and implementing the selection process—identifying and obtaining tools, arranging for personal examination of materials, and involving others in the decision making;
8. Participating in resource sharing through networking and coordinated collection development;
9. Establishing acquisition policies and procedures (that is, guidelines for obtaining materials);
10. Setting up the maintenance program; and
11. Evaluating the collection (p. 23).

While the school library media specialist will be solely responsible for most of these tasks, school district policies will determine the budget, available staff, and the physical facility. A good collection development policy will serve as a guide. Such policies may contain information on the school's mission, how the collection supports the school's mission, who makes selection decisions, criteria used for selection (including acceptance of gifts), use of reviewing sources, weeding, and procedures for handling challenged materials. A good policy can provide protection as well as continuity and clarity about procedures. If the school does not have a collection policy that has been approved by the school board, resources are listed at the end of the chapter where sample policies can be located and modified.

Divergent Perspectives

Because the collection is highly visible, expensive, and interactive, many issues surround it. Some related topics are covered in the chapters on Virtual Libraries and Computerized Reading Management Programs. The focus of this chapter is on the responsibility for selection, the needs of the curriculum, and students' personal interests, classroom collections, censorship, and funding.

■ Responsibility for Selection

Responsibility for selection of the library's materials is spelled out in the school's collection development policy (if one exists). It may specify that the school library media specialist bears primary responsibility, or it could state that the responsibility falls to administrators who then delegate the job to the school media professional staff. In some instances, committees, which include community members, help select materials.

Information Power (AASL/AECT, 1998), the national guidelines for school library media programs, recommends that collections be developed and evaluated collaboratively with teachers to support the school's curriculum and to meet the diverse learning needs of students. Involving teachers in materials selection process for the library media center collection may encourage them to use the library more with their students. They will become familiar with the collection and thus promote information literacy.

On the negative side, teachers do not normally receive the training that school library media specialists do in selecting and evaluating suitable resources for library collections. Teachers could rely heavily on publishers' catalogs rather than review sources. If this happens, you may have to locate some reviews for materials selected by the teacher from catalogs and discuss them with that teacher. A minority of teachers may want to be heavily involved in helping to select materials, others will want no involvement, and some may be too shy to step forward. This could result in an imbalanced collection. Worse, teachers could misinterpret the school media specialist's attempts at involving them in selection as neglecting his or her own duties. Handling teachers in the selection process requires finesse.

The Internet brings another set of issues to the selection process. Teachers have the capability to set up their own Web pages with links to resources or bookmark sites they would like students to use for classroom assignments. The potential exists for the library print collection to be bypassed and mediocre sites chosen. Some schools have technology policies requiring committee approval before teacher Web sites can be changed. If this isn't the case, teachers can be instructed in methods to critically evaluate Web sites using the numerous guides available. In any case, teachers should be made aware of the expertise the school library media specialist can bring to integrating electronic and print resources into the curriculum.

■ Classroom Collections

A classroom collection, or classroom library, can enhance or detract from the school library media center. The collection can enhance the school library media center when the materials housed there extend the library's activities. For example, a classroom collection can provide multiple copies of the library's popular titles. School library media specialists can also pull together materials from the library's shelves for temporary classroom collections when students need extra time to work on special projects. Rather than have one or two classes monopolize the library media center's space, students can continue work in the classroom and free up the center for other students. Classroom collections can work to foster collaboration and communication between teachers and the school library media specialist when each is aware of the other's materials.

Sometimes, classroom libraries develop from materials that have been removed, or weeded, from the school library media center's collections. Conversation on LM_NET has centered on the risky practice of teachers taking weeded items from the school library media center for their classroom libraries. One school media specialist reported that several teachers carted off boxes of these and she heard one comment, "This is great, my students won't need to come to the library!" If items are removed from the school library media center because the information is dated or inaccurate, it should not be made available in the classroom.

With classroom collections, no method exists to manage access and determine the location of books in the school. If a second grader wanted to find out about dolphins, but the only book on dolphins is in the third grade classroom, he or she wouldn't know about it. There is no central catalog or circulation system. Materials get lost. Individual classroom libraries could also duplicate resources and, therefore, waste funds.

In 2001, New York City appropriated funds for each elementary school classroom to buy 300 books. The *New York Times* (Goodnough, 2001) reported several problems. Who would choose the titles and assure proper delivery? Would each classroom have room for the books, and would each teacher know how to incorporate them into lessons? Because few elementary schools in New York City have school library media specialists, classroom teachers will not have assistance with these issues. With reliance on classroom libraries, there is a real risk of never hiring school library media specialists and developing comprehensive school library media centers.

■ Curricular Needs and Personal Interests

The primary role of a school library media center collection is to support the school's curriculum, but it has an equally important role to support the personal interests of students and to instill a love of reading. Accomplishing each of these roles requires purchasing a wide range of materials.

Faced with limited budgets, some school library media specialists believe buying popular materials such as series books, best sellers, and magazines is a waste of library funds. Deeming such materials to have no literary value, they buy only classics and award-winning literature. There is also the argument that many series books (Goosebumps, for example) contain stereotypes and do not encourage critical thinking or build language skills. School library media specialists feel it is their job to steer students away from this type of literature and guide them toward books with more literary merit.

Advocates for including popular literature in the collection claim that free, voluntary reading is enhanced when the school library media specialist provides access to books of varying quality and format and allows the library users to choose their own reading material. Stephen Krashen (1993) refers to studies that support the assertion that the greater the exposure to all types of reading material, the greater the amount of reading that will result.

School library media centers can be viewed as responsive to their users' needs if this type of reading material is represented in the school library collection. School library media centers in rural areas will have to house more popular materials than those in urban areas where students do not have easy access to public library collections.

■ Censorship and Selection

The word censorship is loaded with negative connotations. School library media specialists are generally open minded and promote all views. The American Library Association (2000) has a strong "Freedom to Read" statement that condemns attempts at suppression and pressure to conform directed at libraries from outside groups. As materials are selected and maintained for school library media centers, these ideals should be upheld.

Providing open access to materials with varying views for children is often a balancing act between students' curiosity and the desire of administrators and outside groups to control what is on the library media center's shelves. To avoid confrontations, some school library media specialists do not select materials they believe will cause controversy. This is self-censorship and not selection.

The National Council of Teachers of English (2002) compares censorship and selection:

Censorship	Selection
Is essentially negative	Is essentially affirmative
Seeks to exclude	Seeks to include
Intends to indoctrinate	Intends to educate
Looks at parts of a work in isolation	Looks at the work as a whole

Censorship also takes the form of limiting access to resources in the collection. "Access to Resources and Services in the School Library Media Program: An Interpretation of the Library Bill of Rights" addresses the issue of imposing restrictions on materials: "Major barriers between students and resources include: imposing age or grade level restrictions on the use of resources, limiting the use of interlibrary loan and access to electronic information, charging fees for information in specific formats, requiring permission from parents or teachers, establishing restricted shelves or closed collections, and labeling" (AASL, 2000). School library media specialists who impose these barriers, despite national recommendations, justify their actions in the following ways:

- ▶ We have a K–8 school and there are books that are suitable for the older students and unsuitable for younger students. I maintain separate areas of shelving for the various age groups. I don't want to spend my day being a policeman.
- ▶ I draw black bikinis on pictures of prehistoric men and women in books because they gross me out. I have my limits and believe that children and teenagers should have some limits set too.
- ▶ I place materials that are sure to cause a problem on a "mature" shelf.
- ▶ I note in the online catalog to ask the librarian for the item.
- ▶ Buying materials that have positive reviews that were questionable has burned me.
- ▶ ALA doesn't address the real world.

The majority of school library media specialists begin their jobs with inherited collections. Few have the opportunity to select every title on the shelves. Occasionally, you will run across a book that should not be there. Hopefully, you will familiarize yourself with the collection and eventually make the necessary adjustments. If a parent complains about an item, the collection policy should have the procedure in place for handling the complaint.

■ Funding for the Collection

"A media specialist's professional responsibilities include obtaining funding that will support and strengthen a collection. This may mean presenting facts about the collection, noting its condition, anticipating replacement costs...or seeking outside funding through grants. Soliciting free materials, for example, review copies from journals or publishers, is not selection, it is begging" (Van Orden, 1995, p. 52) School library media specialists with limited budgets often resort to outside fund raising in the form of book fairs, birthday books, and bake sales as supplements. Sometimes, thousands of dollars are raised. However, the drawback to planning such events is time taken away from professional duties. When this type of fund raising is necessary, it is better to have it run by parent volunteers who focus the fund raising on one special item or program rather than the entire collection.

There are dangers in becoming "too good" at raising funds from sales and even grants. Your principal, concluding that you can be counted on to raise your own library budget, could divert monies from what has been appropriated to your program from the school's funds to another teacher or department. Faculty members, feeling that you are making the rest of them "look bad" by getting involved in fund-raising activities, may become resentful. These attitudes from faculty could potentially be tempered by involving them in developing grant proposals or in the decisions as to where extra funds are spent.

Budgets that once only had to support buying library books are now stretched to include technology. In some schools, this could include computers as well as online subscriptions. For example, in the Washington, D.C. area school libraries have seen their budgets shrink with pots of money formerly dedicated to library materials being diverted to computers and new technology (Trejos, 2000). As a result, the amount of money spent per pupil on library books in the Washington area varies widely. In 1998, it ranged from 92 cents per pupil in Baltimore City to $19.34 in Worcester County, according to the Maryland Department of Education. In Montgomery County, spending on library materials fell in 1998 to $5.89 per pupil, down $19.26 from the previous year.

School library media specialists need to educate their administrators on the added expenses of technology. Some administrators believe that books and periodicals won't be needed and "everything can be found on the Internet." Often, a simple hands-on demonstration will convince the administrator this isn't the case. Another strategy is to present administrators with average expenditures figures for school library media center collections (Miller & Shontz, 2001), noting the differences between national averages and your own budget in the areas of electronic and print resources.

Collection development in a school library media center is a balancing act between curricular and popular materials; print and electronic resources; classroom and library; and finding the funds to accomplish it all well. An awareness of the issues surrounding school library media center collections will facilitate this task to a great extent.

Questions for Discussion and Reflection

1. Think back to your own school library media center when you were a student. What is your recollection of the collection? How did you use it?

2. Talk about any personal experiences you have encountered with censorship.

3. What are the criteria that would make a Web site a good informational source for a school library media center?

4. Argue some additional pros and cons on fund raising for school library media center collections.

5. Should a school library media center present all views on all subjects?

Projects

1. Work with a teacher or teacher-in-training and choose a topic for a typical unit taught in the schools. Utilize reviewing guides suggested in *The Collection Program in Schools* (Van Orden & Bishop, 2001) to select the best resources to support the unit that include books, audiovisual materials, and electronic sources. Limit your spending to five hundred dollars.

2. Make a presentation based on Stephen Krashen's research and the implications that it has on school library media center collection development.

3. Visit a school and get permission to observe some classrooms. Check to see if classroom libraries are available. Interview the teachers, students, and a school library media specialist about how the classroom libraries are used.

References

American Association of School Librarians. (2000). *Access to resources and services in the school library media programs: An interpretation of the Library Bill of Rights*. Retrieved July 8, 2003, from <www.ala.org/aasl/positions/ps_billofrights.html>.

American Association of School Librarians, & Association for Educational Communications and Technology. (1998). *Information power: Building partnerships for learning*. Chicago: American Library Association.

American Library Association, & Association of American Publishers. (2000). *The freedom to read statement*. Retrieved July 8, 2003 from <www.ala.org/alaorg/oif/freeread.html>.

Goodnough, A. (2001, May 30). How to make 2100 classroom libraries. *The New York Times*, B9.

Krashen, S.D. (1993). *The power of reading: Insights from the research*. Englewood, CO: Libraries Unlimited.

Miller, M., & Shontz, M. (2001, October). New money, old books. *School Library Journal 47* (10), 50–60.

The National Council of Teachers of English. (2002, November). *Anticensorship: Get help!*. Retrieved July 8, 2003, from <www.ncte.org/censorship/>.

Trejos, N. (2000, January 31). Lamenting libraries: Budget cuts, internet access deplete schools' book supply. *The Washington Post*, B1.

Van Orden, P.J. (1995). *The collection program in schools: Concepts, practices, and information sources*. Englewood, CO: Libraries Unlimited.

Van Orden, P.J. & Bishop G.K. (2001). *The collection program in schools: Concepts, practices, and information sources*. Englewood, CO: Libraries Unlimited.

Additional Information

American Library Association. (1998). *Workbook for selection policy writing*. Retrieved July 8, 2003, from American Library Association, Office for Intellectual Freedom Web site at <www.ala.org/alaorg/oif/workbook_selection.html>.

Callison, D. (1990, Fall): A review of the research related to school library media collections: part I [Electronic Version]. *School Library Media Quarterly, 19* (1).

Manning, P. (1997, May). When less is more: Cultivating a healthy collection. *School Library Journal, 43* (5), 54–55.

Miller, M., & Shontz, M.L. (2000, November). Location is everything. *School Library Journal, 46* (11), 57–67.

Reichman, H. (2001). *Censorship and selection: Questions and answers for schools.* 3rd ed. Chicago: American Library Association.

Van Orden, P.J. (2000). *Selecting books for the elementary school library media center: A complete guide.* New York: Neal-Schuman.

Web Sites

Resource Guides for School Library Media Program Development: Collection Development
    <www.ala.org/aasl/resources/collection.html>
    Presents links to review sources, articles, materials lists for collection development by the American Association of School Librarians.

Sunlink's "Weed of the Month"
    <www.sunlink.ucf.edu/weed/>
    Detailed instructions on how to weed a school collection in a particular subject area is supplied each month. Archives can be accessed for previous subjects.

Kathy Schrock's Guide for Educators: Teacher Helpers — Critical Evaluation Information
    <school.discovery.com/schrockguide/eval.html>
    Provides a series of Web evaluation guides for elementary, middle, and high school levels as well as links to articles about Web site evaluation.

Computerized Reading Management Programs

Computerized reading management programs are today's hi-tech answer to the book report. This is how they work. Students select a book from a recommended list. Point values are assigned to each book based on its reading difficulty. Once the student reads a book, he or she goes to the computer and takes a multiple-choice test about important facts in the book. The computer scores the test, awards the student points based on test performance, and keeps a complete record of results. Students get feedback on how they did immediately; teachers can request reports at any time. The software required to run the program consists of an overall student management system module as well as individual disks of titles arranged by grade/reading levels and subject themes. Often administered school-wide by the school library media specialist, the programs can be used in individual classrooms as well.

The major programs presently on the market are *Accelerated Reader*, produced by Renaissance Learning (2003), and *Reading Counts*, produced by Scholastic (2003). *Book Adventure* (Book Adventure Foundation, 2003), another alternative, elicits corporate sponsors to support a free Web-based product. Each claims to motivate children to read and improve their comprehension.

Although all achieve the same testing goals, some significant differences exist in each of the programs (Everhart, 1998). Programs vary on numerous characteristics: price, network capabilities, number of titles for which quizzes are available (fiction and nonfiction), types of reports available, computer requirements, ability to create your own quizzes, customer support, training, and more. Each manufacturer is constantly updating these features so be sure to compare the most current version of the programs. For example, a recent upgrade to *Accelerated Reader* allows for emergent readers to hear questions and answer choices audibly as well as visually.

What about cheating? Can't a student just watch a video or read a summary of the book to pass a test? Probably not. Each manufacturer is careful to incorporate questions that could not be answered by watching a video. Moreover, the number of questions in a quiz makes it highly unlikely that simply reading a jacket summary will attain a passing score. *Reading Counts* stores 30 questions for each book in a test bank and then generates ten random questions so that no two students receive the same quiz (and pass on the answers). *Accelerated Reader* creates the same ten-question quiz for each student, although the order of answer choices is scrambled.

Divergent Perspectives

Several issues surrounding computerized reading management programs and their use in school library media centers have sparked debate within the profession. They include: motivation and rewards, book selection, library collections and budgets, staff time, and raising reading test scores and research.

■ Motivation and Rewards

An outgrowth of assigning point values to books and keeping track of student point totals is students earning rewards as they reach specified point levels. Whether or not to reward students and the types of rewards given are decisions made by the school but are not prerequisites of installing a computerized reading management program.

Those promoting rewards maintain they motivate students to read more books. But how? There are two types of motivation—intrinsic and extrinsic. Intrinsic motivation is being motivated and curious to do an activity for its own sake. Extrinsic motivation refers to being motivated in an activity as a means to an end, such as receiving a reward or because someone tells you to do the activity. Critics believe rewards only motivate extrinsically. Proponents theorize that the rewards will jump start reluctant readers extrinsically at first but instill an intrinsic motivation as they read more (Everhart, 1999).

Closely related to intrinsic and extrinsic motivation is the concept of tangible and intangible rewards. Tangible rewards can be of a physical nature such as candy, prizes, or money, or they can also be grades or recognition. Intangible rewards include verbal praise, interaction, and discussion. Educators overseeing computerized reading management programs implement a wide variety of rewards ranging from posting names for points earned in prominent places to setting up stores where students can spend "book bucks." These stores are stocked with everything from McDonald's coupons to boom boxes. Both *Accelerated Reader* and *Reading Counts* have incentive products available in their catalogs that include clothing, certificates, medals, and sporting goods emblazoned with their logo. Some schools depend on small budget items such as bulk candy, erasers, pencils, and bookmarks for rewards. *Book Adventure's* Web site requires kids to obtain teacher or parent verification to redeem their points for prizes. Prizes consist of food coupons to chain restaurants, CDs, magazine subscriptions, games, and stickers.

> A popular ploy, which costs nothing, is to have the principal engage in an outrageous act once the entire school meets an accumulated point goal. Principals shaving their heads, kissing a pig, and conducting business from the roof for a day, have been reported to incite kids to read thousands of books (Everhart, 1998).

Several experts have criticized using rewards to motivate students to read because the focus is on rewards rather than reading. Alfie Kohn, author of *Punished by Rewards* (1993), maintains that tangible rewards lead to diminished motivation as children choose short, simple books to read in order to get the reward. One of the most outspoken critics of computerized reading management programs, Dr. Betty Carter of Texas Women's University's School of Library and Information Studies, agrees with these reasons and offers a few more. Carter (1996) asserts that the use of rewards, so often coupled with these programs, actually devalues reading. "By granting rewards for reading more and supposedly better books, educators unconsciously make a public statement: Reading cannot stand alone as an enjoyable pursuit. When they offer bonuses for reading, educators not only deliver an unappealing message, they also lessen the possibility that children will read voluntarily" (p. 23).

School library media specialists, like Carol Buchanan (1997) at the Bedminster Township School in New Jersey and an *Accelerated Reader* user, disagrees. "For some children, this extrinsic motivation works. It does not necessarily mean we are giving incentives for a less-than-desirable task. Rather, we are giving rewards for a job well done. Although in my middle-class community where students own expensive video and computer games, skateboards, and roller blades, the rewards we give are rather meager. Oftentimes the satisfaction lies in completing a book (sometimes for the first time!), being able to answer some questions about the book, and seeing those points accumulate!" (p. 8).

■ Book Selection

Another criticism of using computerized reading management programs is that students confine their reading to only the books in the test database, passing up good quality literature on the shelves. Or, they read a larger number of easier books to accumulate points. School library media specialists complain that students don't know how to browse for or select books to read for pleasure, choosing a book based solely on the number of points it carries. Students have trouble discussing books and going beyond the level of simply answering multiple-choice questions. They are not encouraged to think but rather to regurgitate facts.

Students involved in a five-year study of *Accelerated Reader* (Peak & Dewalt, 1993), felt that *Accelerated Reader* helped increase their overall vocabulary and they actually read more and better books. Students liked not having to write conventional book reports as well as the fairness and accuracy of the system and the immediate reinforcement they received.

Some educators believe students would not read at all if they did not have the requirement imposed by a formal reading program. Their philosophy? Even if students are reading simplistic books, at least they are reading.

■ Library Collections and Budgets

School library media specialists report that students read more and library circulation increases when a school has a computerized reading management program (Renaissance Learning, Inc., 2003). The increased circulation has resulted in some school library media centers being allotted more money for books. Well-managed programs also generate excitement in students and parents, which can bring attention and funding to the school library media center.

Other schools are not as fortunate. Miller and Shontz (1997) reported a negative impact of computerized reading management programs on budgets and collection development. Twenty-three percent of participating school library media centers spend 61% to 100% of their budgets on books required by these programs. School library media centers with small budgets may only have enough money to purchase these companion books each year. As a result, collection development is taken out of the hands of the school library media specialist. Schools are also purchasing books that would not meet previously established selection criteria only because they are part of the test database.

■ Staff Time

Many activities can be associated with running a computerized reading program including labeling books, altering catalog records, running reports, installing software, updating student information, providing motivational prizes, and producing reading lists to name a few. All these activities take up staff time. Those considering the systems should carefully consider the added workload.

Some school library media specialists feel the added workload is justified when they see children reading more books. They also enlist the help of student and parent volunteers for some of the tasks, especially if a reward system is in place.

■ Raising Reading Test Scores and Research

Sales and advertising literature for both *Accelerated Reader* and *Reading Counts* are teeming with claims that using their software will raise students' scores on standardized tests. With all the emphasis on test scores at both the state and national levels, schools are grasping at these programs to provide a quick fix. Anxious administrators have been known to purchase a program and have it installed on a school's network or in the library media center unbeknownst to the school library media specialist. Library media specialists are directed to manage school-wide programs with no background or training. Or sometimes school media professionals are left "out of the loop" altogether.

There is substantial "research" available about test scores cited in corporate sales literature. One word of caution—the company marketing the product may have conducted some of the research. *Accelerated Reader's* manufacturer, Renaissance Learning, actually funds the School Renaissance Institute—the producer of numerous studies linking

Accelerated Reader to higher reading scores in standardized tests. At its Independent Research Web site, there is a searchable database of research conducted by outside groups as well as its own company (Renaissance Learning, Inc., 2003).

A sampling of unbiased studies has been cited throughout this chapter. Others are listed in the section on Additional Information. An excellent example of an independent study is one conducted by Dr. Keith Topping (1999), *Formative Assessment of Reading Comprehension by Computer: Advantages and Disadvantages of The Accelerated Reader Software*. He concluded, "Whatever its advantages, Accelerated Reader is not a substitute for balanced reading instruction. Rather, it is intended as a supplementary and complementary resource — albeit a powerful one under the right circumstances — that can help the teacher deliver the curriculum effectively. These conclusions have implications for local, state, and national guidelines on literacy instruction that aim to raise teacher effectiveness and standards of achievement. Placing intelligent software in classrooms does not guarantee it will be used intelligently."

Questions for Discussion and Reflection

1. What if your principal suddenly announced that he or she was installing a computerized reading management program in the library media center at the beginning of the next school year? What would you do?

2. Discuss the pros and cons of using the free Web-based program, *Book Adventure*, vs. the locally installed *Accelerated Reader*, which is a pay program.

3. What strategies could you use to ensure that buying books for a computerized reading management program did not consume your entire book budget?

4. How would you manage rewards if you were running a computerized reading management program?

5. How would you work with students, faculty, and administration to overcome a situation where students are only reading books in the test database?

Projects

1. Visit a school library media center that has installed a computerized reading management program. Interview the school library media specialist about the impact of the program on: the library budget, collection development, student test scores, circulation, staff workload and other topics discussed in this chapter.

2. Obtain demo software and product literature for both *Accelerated Reader* and *Reading Counts*. Compare and contrast their features. Choose the one you would purchase for your library media center. Justify your answer.

3. Prepare a proposal for implementing a computerized reading program in your library media center that you would present to your administration. Include the following components: benefits of installing the program, three-year budget for books, hardware, and software, and plans for educating students, faculty, and parents.

References

The Book Adventure Foundation. (2002). *Book Adventure*. Retrieved July 8, 2003, from <www.bookadventure.org>.

Buchanan, C. (1997, January). Letters. *School Library Journal 43* (1), 6, 8.

Carter, B. (1996, October). Hold the applause. *School Library Journal, 42* (10), 22–25.

Everhart, N.L. (1998, January). Virtual book reports [Electronic version]. *Electronic School 3*, 22–26. Retrieved March 3, 2003, from <www.electronic-school.com/0198f3.html>.

Everhart, N.L. (1999, March/April). Reading motivation: An analysis of computerized reading programs in relationship to motivational research. *Knowledge Quest 27* (4), 18–24.

Kohn, A. (1995). *Punished by rewards*. New York: Houghton Mifflin.

Miller, M. L., & Schontz, M. L. (1997, October). Small change: Expenditures for resources in school library media centers FY 95–96. *School Library Journal, 43* (10), 28–37.

Peak, J., & Dewalt, M.W. (1993). *Effects of the Computerized Accelerated Reader Program on Reading Achievement*. Paper presented at the Annual Meeting of the Eastern Educational Research Association, Clearwater Beach, FL. (ERIC Document Reproduction Service No. ED363269).

Renaissance Learning, Inc. (2003). *Accelerated Reader overview*. Retrieved July 8, 2003, from <www.renlearn.com/ar/default.htm>.

Renaissance Learning, Inc. (2003). *Success stories and research*. Retrieved July 8, 2003, from <research.renlearn.com>.

Scholastic, Inc. (2001). *Welcome to Scholastic Reading Counts!* Retrieved July 8, 2003, from <src.scholastic.com/ecatalog/readingcounts/index.htm>.

Topping, K. (1999). Formative assessment of reading comprehension by computer: Advantages and disadvantages of The *Accelerated Reader* Software. *International Reading Association*. Retrieved July 8, 2003, from <www.readingonline.org/critical/topping/>.

Additional Information

Hamilton, B. (1997, March/April). Using Accelerated Reader with ESL students. *Multimedia Schools, 4* (2), 50–52.

Poock, M. (1998, May). The Accelerated Reader: An analysis of the software's strengths and weaknesses and how it can be used to its best potential. *School Library Media Activities Monthly, 14* (9), 32–35.

Vollands, S., & Others. (1996). *Experimental evaluation of computer assisted self-assessment of reading comprehension: Effects on reading achievement and attitude.* Scotland, United Kingdom: Centre for Paired Learning. (ERIC Document Reproduction Service No. ED408567).

Web Sites

Accelerated Reading Chatboard
<teachers.net/mentors/accelerated_reading/>
An independent discussion forum dedicated to teachers utilizing Accelerated Reading programs in the classroom.

Reading Matters
<www.nea.org/reading/research-reading.html>
Sponsored by the National Education Association, this site provides extensive links to research reports on reading for teachers and parents.

Scheduling

The method in which classes are scheduled to use the school library media center can significantly influence several vital components of the school library media program—the level of collaboration between the school library media specialist and teachers, the retention of skills by students, and even the variety and depth of services offered.

Currently, there are three types of schedules in place in school library media centers—fixed, flexible, and block (and combinations thereof). In a fixed schedule, classes visit the school library media center during the same period each week. It is common for the classroom teacher to send or drop his or her students off at the library media center and use this time as a planning or "prep" period. While the students are in the library during their scheduled or "fixed" time, the school library media specialist may teach information literacy classes, conduct story-time, or monitor book exchanges, depending on the curriculum and grade level. Sometimes, the school librarian is responsible for assigning a library grade to students with fixed library times.

A flexible schedule is just as its sounds—flexible. Students are scheduled to use the school library media center as the need arises. They may spend several days in a row in the library, researching for information to support a class unit as their teacher and the school library media specialist work side by side with them. Or, weeks may go by before they need to use the services of the school library media center. In addition to visiting the library as an entire class, students come in small groups and individually.

Fixed scheduling is dominant in elementary schools—slightly more than half of elementary schools use this method. Approximately 40% use a combination of fixed and flexible scheduling. Fixed scheduling is used less in middle and high schools. Flexible and combination scheduling is dominant in middle schools, where approximately 48% use flexible scheduling and an equal share use a combination of fixed and flexible scheduling. Flexible scheduling is also dominant in high schools. Eighty-four percent of high schools use flexible scheduling; only 4% use fixed scheduling (McKracken, 2001).

Block scheduling, also employed mostly at the secondary level, combines several class periods into a "block." In doing so, it is predicted that students will benefit from more intensive learning activities with more time for following through on assignments.

Block scheduling is a relatively new concept prompted by the report, *Prisoners of Time* (National Education Commission on Time and Learning, 1994). In that report, reformers declared that time is the enemy of today's secondary schools because students barely have enough time to get involved in a class before they must move to the next one. They stated: "We have been asking the impossible of our students—that they learn as much as their foreign peers while spending only half as much time in core academic subjects" (p.8).

Divergent Perspectives

The argument of fixed vs. flexible scheduling is one of the oldest and most persistent in the profession. Although there is a general consensus that flexible scheduling is more appropriate, some recent publications have generated support for fixed scheduling. Block scheduling is another issue confronting school library media specialists.

■ Flexible Scheduling

Flexible scheduling is widely accepted in the profession. In *Information Power* (1998), the national guidelines for school library media programs, flexible scheduling is strongly advocated. The American Association of School Librarians (2000) in its "Position Statement on Flexible Scheduling" makes the point that the library media program should be fully integrated into the school and in order for this to happen; a flexible schedule must be maintained. This is supported in research by Tallman and van Deusen (1995) where they found that flexible scheduling improves the likelihood of curriculum consultation by the library media specialist. The researchers also offer the following generalizations based on their study of scheduling for consideration:

- ▶ Principals who expected teacher/library media specialist collaboration had media programs that were more than ancillary. This underscored the importance of principals having an understanding of the benefits of collaboration between teachers and library media specialists.
- ▶ The time media specialists spent in meeting with teachers led to more extensive involvement within a curriculum unit.
- ▶ Library media specialists meeting with teams of teachers yielded more curriculum involvement than meeting with teachers individually. Perhaps the teachers who work in teams are already disposed toward collaboration, and so working with the library media specialists is natural.
- ▶ More consultation activity was reported from schools characterized by flexible or mixed scheduling than from those characterized by fixed scheduling
- ▶ If flexible scheduling was employed, significant differences in consultations occurred between full-time library media specialists and part-time ones, but these differences were not evident in fixed or mixed scheduling sites.

The previously mentioned McKracken (2001) study also shows that there is a correlation between the type of scheduling used and the ability to practice the roles as described in *Information Power*. Elementary school library media specialists who use flexible scheduling perceive they are able to practice more roles than library media specialists who use either combination or fixed scheduling. Those who used fixed scheduling perceive they are able to implement fewer roles than those who use either combination or flexible scheduling.

The importance of flexible scheduling was illustrated in the national *Library Power* program. This program provided millions of dollars to improve school libraries in cities throughout the United States in the late 1980s through the early 1990s. In order for schools to qualify for *Library Power* funding, they had to commit to a flexibly scheduled school library media program with a full-time certified school librarian. In the *Executive Summary: Findings from the Evaluation of the National Library Power Program* (DeWitt Wallace Reader's Digest Fund, 1999), it was also reported that the transition to a flexible access program allowed for more collaboration between teachers and the school library media specialist as well as increased use of the library by the students.

Jan Buchanan (1991) also summarizes the benefits of flexible scheduling in her book, *Flexible Access Library Media Programs*:

> ▶ Teachers can take advantage of the spontaneity of the teachable moment and send students to the school library media center when interest is high;
> ▶ Teachers can collaborate with the school library media specialist for team teaching and collaboratively developed units;
> ▶ Teachers can work with the school library media specialists to integrate the *Information Literacy Standards for Student Learning* into the curriculum of the classroom;
> ▶ Students learn research and information literacy skills they will use as lifelong learners;
> ▶ Students become independent users of resources;
> ▶ Students interact with other students and teachers from different classes and grade levels; and
> ▶ Students develop a sense of responsibility for their own learning.

Although the benefits of flexible scheduling are many, the main barrier to it in elementary schools is that that the fixed time is often used as a teacher's planning time. Although this time may be mandated contractually to be provided it is not mandated that the school library media program provide the time. Strategies to overcome this time barrier and plan for flexible access include (Hughes-Hassell & Whelock, 2001):

> ▶ Rearranging the school library media center to allow for large groups, small groups, and individuals to use the school library media center simultaneously;
> ▶ Developing new schedules so teachers can sign up to use the school library media center for both small group and whole class instruction;
> ▶ Establishing procedures for checkout; and
> ▶ Developing an implementation timetable.

The authors (Hughes-Hassell & Whelock, 2001) also provide solid answers to questions that will undoubtedly be asked by administrators and teachers as school library media specialists attempt to implement flexible scheduling.

■ Fixed Scheduling

Most school library media specialists support the concept of flexible scheduling. If flexible scheduling is not already being practiced in their schools, they are working towards that goal. However, little has been written in the literature about the benefits of fixed scheduling. It might be almost heresy to cite any benefits, but that is what Doug Johnson (2001) did in an opinion piece, "It's Good to be Inflexible" in *School Library Journal*. It is printed here in its entirety with permission.

> Look, I'm tired of getting beat up about our fixed schedule library media programs. I've offered my last apology. I know the American Association of School Librarians (AASL) through its position papers, standards, and editorial policies says in no uncertain terms that flexibly scheduled library programs are good and programs with fixed library schedules are bad. Granted there is some research about the benefits of flexibly scheduled programs, and anytime we can work toward proven best practices, we should.
>
> But unfortunately what many dedicated professionals hear is: "School media specialists in flexibly scheduled programs are good and school media specialists in programs with fixed schedules are bad." This one-sided philosophy takes the wind out of the many media specialists' sails who are in fixed schedules. Is there no room in the AASL tent for both the flexible and the fixed? I believe there are some serious downsides to flexible scheduling and strengths to fixed scheduling that I can't find addressed in the literature:
>
> 1. **You can't teach kids you don't see.** I've never met a media specialist in a flex program that meets with every teacher on staff, let alone for an equal amount of time. Granted those students whose teacher is cooperative get a superior learning experience. But what about the kids whose teachers are so isolationist that they don't even get

to the library for book checkout, let alone to learn media skills? Shouldn't we be asking: Do we give some kids great skills and other kids no skills, or do we give all kids the ability to learn some skills knowing that we could do better in an ideal world?

2. **We are enabling teachers to deviate from the curriculum.** High-stakes testing will be a fixed mountain in our political landscape for some time, like it or not. One benefit of testing has been to standardize our curriculum to make sure all teachers actually teach the skills they are expected to teach. Unless "flexible" scheduling is mandated for every class, it encourages the rogue-teacher mentality of teaching: "what I want to teach and when I want to teach it." Shouldn't we be asking: Does a flexible or fixed schedule work better with a prescribed curriculum?

3. **It's not just research, but reading.** The library media program's emphasis on improving reading skills by encouraging independent reading practice may prove to be the hobbit that saves us from the goblins looking for "nonessential" programs to whack. Every child deserves time every week to experience story times, book talks, and, for goodness sake, book check out! Shouldn't we be asking: Do we sacrifice our role in promoting lifelong readers that can be best done with regular library media center visits to our role in teaching technology and information literacy skills in flexibly scheduled programs?

4. **Inquiry should be a daily activity.** Flexible scheduling seems to encourage teachers and media specialists to work together on only big projects during the school year. But how accurately does this reflect how adults conduct inquiry? Most of us do little bitty inquiry "projects" every day. (Where do I get the best price on that lawn mower?) Weekly mini-lessons that apply a single aspect of the inquiry process, tied to a class topic, may well provide better practice in real problem solving. Shouldn't we be asking: Can smaller but continuous opportunities for practicing information literacy skills be as or more beneficial than a few, isolated larger projects?

5. **We are neglecting our part in the containment agreement.** Schools have three charges from society: teach, socialize, and contain. Yes, keeping an eye on the community's young people while Mom and Dad are working. When media specialists in a fixed schedule also provide prep time, they are helping hold up the containment part of school's obligation. And let's just get bottom-line pragmatic — it's hard to fire prep-time providers. Shouldn't we be asking: Do we want to work with a fixed schedule and have job security or with a flex schedule and be vulnerable to cuts?

   Like it or not, we operate in a real world with budgets, differing teaching styles, and community expectations that impinge on our professional dignity. All good professionals play the best game they can with the cards they're been dealt and never let a fixed schedule be an excuse for an ineffective program. Come on, AASL, take the blinders off. (Johnson, D., 2001, p. 39).

Needless to say, Johnson's piece was controversial (on his Web site, <www.doug-johnson.com>, he jokingly remarks that it will get him thrown out of the profession). But many of the responses (Johnson, 2003) brought supporters of fixed scheduling "out of the closet."

Some additional positive and negative aspects of fixed scheduling cited by practicing school library media specialists are:

POSITIVE

▶ They choose to have fixed schedules because it ensures that they see every student. They note that a flexible schedule sounds great in theory but after doing it discovered that either they were frazzled with too many projects/classes or bored looking for things to do.

▶ Fixed scheduling works best when you have to visit several schools. On a flexible schedule it is just too difficult to try and plan with teachers in multiple buildings.

NEGATIVE

▶ There's not enough time to accomplish what needs to be done as books are also checked out during that time.
▶ The school library media specialist isn't available to help individual students with book selection or research because he or she is too busy teaching skills in isolation.
▶ The students are not graded on library skills causing discipline and attention problems.

Fixed scheduling could be successful because of extenuating factors, such as small school populations or larger facility sizes, and not inherently due to the schedule itself. Certain school library media specialists with very small schools, thus a limited number of fixed classes, seem to like fixed scheduling because there are still enough periods to have flexible time. A larger facility, and helpful support staff, can accommodate fixed classes working with the school library media specialist, while aides and volunteers run the circulation desk for other students.

■ Combining Fixed and Flexible Scheduling

Creative school library media specialists have combined fixed and flexible scheduling in their programs. Many feel that seeing very young children in elementary school helps to set the tone of the library program, thus facilitating library usage later on. Here are some scenarios illustrating combined scheduling:

▶ Primary (K–3) students are scheduled in, while grades four to six are on a flexible schedule. Information skills are integrated into research units. Younger students are introduced to a variety of library skills during the year, but mostly they have a story and book exchange.
▶ A fixed schedule is implemented during the first few weeks of school with the help of the teachers.
▶ Students are seen on a regular basis and most of the time without their help. While giving teachers extra prep-time, it keeps the concept of flex time because the school library media specialist arranges the schedule and allows for integration of curriculum topics.

- A "semi-flex schedule," K–2 weekly, 3–6 alternate weeks, leaves quite a bit of open time which has the following advantages:
  - Provides for open times every week for the voracious readers or the reluctant readers;
  - Provides for small group instruction at a teacher's request;
  - Allows whole classes or individuals to perform research;
  - Assists students who are doing special projects;
  - Allows the class doing a research project to be scheduled into the library three times a week when it really needs it;
  - Provides the younger classes with weekly scheduled visits—they really benefit from a predictable schedule and they get to borrow books weekly; and
  - Assures that older kids receive some instruction in library skills even if their teachers are the kind who would never willingly coordinate with a librarian or schedule the class to go the library.

■ Block Scheduling

Block scheduling provides large "chunks" of time that allows students to do in-depth research. Seven or eight periods per day may be condensed into three or four. "Students may have up to two hours to dig into resources and make substantial progress on research projects. They have the time to locate, select, assess, and interpret information in one "shot." Teachers and library media specialists can take the time to coach several students, giving them adequate time to ask critical questions and follow complex strategies" (Farmer, 1999, p. 18).

A survey of school library media specialists on how block scheduling changed the use of their libraries found both positive and negative changes (Gierke, 1999):

POSITIVE CHANGES
- Increased demand for library services;
- Increased interactive teaching methods and hand-on projects;
- Increased requests for reserved books;
- Provided a wider variety of subject areas being researched;
- Helped the library become the learning lab for the whole school;

- ▶ Provided an opportunity to work with individual students;
- ▶ Allowed enough time to teach electronic information access in depth;
- ▶ Inspired library renovation or new structures to accommodate block scheduling; and
- ▶ Facilitated networking the OPAC and databases into classrooms.

NEGATIVE CHANGES
- ▶ Increases pace of the day;
- ▶ Allows for misuse of time when teachers scheduled the entire block;
- ▶ Takes away time for administrative tasks;
- ▶ Unscheduled visits are impossible when librarians serve multiple classes in each block;
- ▶ Lack of comfort by teachers with change;
- ▶ Some teachers cut back on assigning projects initially to make sure class material was covered;
- ▶ Drops in circulation figures as students use more materials in-house;
- ▶ Decreased opportunities for recreational reading; and
- ▶ Not enough space.

Although there were some negative aspects reported, 85% of the students and teachers surveyed would not choose to return to the former schedule (Gierke, 1999).

Block scheduling can be a catalyst for instructional change within a school and the school library media center can benefit. Teachers who have 90-minute periods may be more eager to collaborate because they are seeking methods to break up the time, individualizing learning, and using multiple resources (Kirschenman, 1998). In order to use the library media center effectively in a block schedule Kirschenman (1998) suggests library media specialists encourage individual research, using the library media center's resources in the classroom, using creative projects, setting up learning stations, using media-skills-based activities, team teaching in the library media center, and using state library, interlibrary loan, CD-ROM, and online materials.

Farmer (1999) elaborates on additional difficulties of a block schedule for teachers using the school library media center with their classes. Problems can arise when several teachers want to sign up for the same block of time. Teachers can no longer work in isolation but need to carefully sequence class time in the library, plan for the availability for resources for all students, and choreograph learning spaces in the library, computer lab, production area, and classroom. Hints for teachers and school library media specialists in managing a block schedule are provided by Teger & Nunn (1999):

Hints for Teachers and Library Media Specialists

DO'S
- Participate in staff development;
- Display weekly schedule of classes in library media center;
- Teach organizational skills;
- Vary activities (active and passive);
- Establish a commitment among the administration and staff to try new instructional activities;
- Remember to get kids actively involved;
- Try interdisciplinary projects;
- Teach in different settings;
- Use media; and
- Be creative.

DON'TS
- Assume that productive passive activities can last more than 30 minutes;
- Underestimate the students' abilities to be flexible;
- Lecture all period;
- Under plan;
- Use more audiovisual resources without integrating into instruction; and
- Allow long student breaks.

Each method of scheduling the school library media center has distinct advantages and disadvantages. It is important for the school library media specialist to be aware of these and work with teachers and administrators in establishing the most conducive learning atmosphere in the school. Although scheduling is extremely important, what may be more important is the quality of collaboration woven throughout that schedule.

Questions for Discussion and Reflection

1. In a flexible schedule, what are some techniques you can use to ensure that all students receive equal access to the school library media center?

2. Describe some additional activities you could incorporate into the school library media center if it was on a block schedule.

3. React to Doug Johnson's arguments in favor of fixed scheduling.

4. What are some strategies you could use to collaborate with teachers if your program was on a fixed schedule and library time was used as the teachers' prep period?

5. List advantages and disadvantages of block, fixed, flexible, and combined scheduling from a teacher's perspective. Do the same from the students' perspective.

Projects

1. Visit three schools with similar demographics but different types of school library media center schedules. Observe each one for a day and write a paper comparing and contrasting your observations.

2. Conduct a survey of schools in your immediate area. Find out what type of schedule is employed in the school library media center and compare it to standardized test scores of students in the school. Report on your findings.

3. Write a report summarizing research studies that have been conducted in the area of school library media center scheduling.

References

American Association of School Librarians. (1998). *Information power: Building partnerships for learning*. Chicago: American Library Association.

American Association of School Librarians. (2000). *Position statement on flexible scheduling*. Retrieved July 8, 2003, from American Association of School Librarians Web site at <www.ala.org/aasl/positions/ps_flexible.html>.

Buchanan, J. (1991). *Flexible access library media programs*. Englewood, CO: Libraries Unlimited.

DeWitt Wallace-Reader's Digest Fund. (1999). *Executive Summary: Findings from the evaluation of the National Library Power Program*. Retrieved July 8, 2003, from DeWitt Wallace-Reader's Digest Fund Web site at <www.wallacefunds.org/publications/pdf/libpowr.pdf>.

Farmer, L.S. (1999, September/October). Making block time for big thinking. *Book Report 18* (2), 18–20.

Gierke, C. (1999, September/October). What's behind block scheduling? *Book Report 18* (2), 8–10.

Hughes-Hassell, S., & Whelock, A. (2001). Flexible access: Essential to active learning. In S. Hughes-Hassell & A. Whelock (Eds.), *The information-powered school* (pp. 83–93). Chicago: American Library Association.

Johnson, D. (2001, November). It's good to be inflexible. *School Library Journal 47* (11), 39.

Johnson, D. (2003). *Homepage for Doug Johnson, author, speaker and consultant on school library media center issues, technology in education, intellectual freedom, information literacy, school facilities planning, staff development, rubrics, computer ethics, and leadership*. Retrieved July 8, 2003, from <www.doug-johnson.com>.

Johnson, D. (2002). *Responses to School Library Journal opinion piece on flexible and fixed scheduling*. Retrieved July 8, 2003, from <www.doug-johnson.com/dougwri/responses.html>.

Kirschenman, J.W. (1998, September). Time is on your side: Library media centers and block scheduling. *School Library Media Activities Monthly (15)* 1, 25–26.

McCracken, A. (2001, June). *School library media specialists' perceptions of practice and importance of roles described in Information Power*. Retrieved July 8, 2003, from American Association of School Librarians Web site at <www.ala.org/Content/NavigationMenu/AASL/Publications_and_Journals/School_Library_Media_Research/Content1/Volume_4_(2001)/McCracken.htm>.

National Education Commission on Time and Learning. (1994). *Prisoners of time: Report of the National Education Commission on Time and Learning*. Washington, DC: United States Government Printing Office.

Tallman, J.I., & Donham van Deusen, J. (1995). Is flexible scheduling always the answer? Some surprising results from a national study. In B.J. Morris (Ed.), *School Library Media Annual* (pp. 201–205). Littleton, CO: Libraries Unlimited.

Teger, N.L., & Nunn, D. (1999, Nov/Dec). Impact of block schedules on library media centers. *Knowledge Quest, 28* (2), 10–11, 13–15.

Additional Information

Donham van Deusen, J. (1999). Prerequisites to flexible scheduling. In K. Haycock (Ed.), *Foundations for effective school library media programs* (pp. 223–227). Englewood, CO: Libraries Unlimited.

Fox, C.J. (2001, Jan/Feb). Designing a flexible schedule for an elementary school library media center. *Library Talk (14)* 1, 10–13.

North Carolina Department of Public Instruction. (1998). *Flexible access to the school library media center: For the children: Bibliography*. Retrieved July 8, 2003, from <video.dpi.state.nc.us/media/flex/Bibliography.html>.

Ohlrich, K.B. (1992, May). Flexible scheduling: The dream vs. reality. *School Library Journal 38* (5), 35–38.

Shannon, D.M. (1996). Tracking the transition to a flexible access library program in two Library Power schools. *School Library Media Quarterly 24* (3), 158–163.

Shaw, M. K. (1999). *Block scheduling and its impact on the school library media center*. Westport, CT: Greenwood Publishing.

Web Sites

Resource Guides for School Library Media Program Development: Flexible Scheduling
<www.ala.org/aasl/resources/flexible.html>
Links to research studies, technical reports, bibliographies and position statements on flexible scheduling.

Facilities

The importance of the space and environment of the school library media center cannot be overstated. The amount of space available in the school library media center, and the way in which it is used, can impact the school library media specialist's ability to achieve the goals set forth for the school library media program. The physical size will determine the number of students who can use the facility at any one time, whether as a class, individually, or in small groups. Obviously, more resources and services can be made available in a larger facility.

Aside from the size and resources available in the school library media center, the "feel" one gets when entering the facility is important. This feel is often referred to as the "climate" of the school library media center. Although the dimensions of the school library media center can't be changed, factors that impact the climate can. Paint, furniture, appropriate signage, curtains, floor treatments, decorations, plants, and more can all be used to create a warm climate. The national Library Power program provided funds to refurbish over 700 school library facilities and improve climate. Teachers and students became drawn to the improved facilities, thus encouraging more effective use (DeWitt Wallace Reader's Digest Fund, 1999).

Likewise, in New York City, the Robin Hood Foundation has enlisted the help of some of the country's best architects and school library consultants to design warm and inviting school library media centers for the city's 656 elementary schools. By focusing on library facilities, the organization is hoping to boost student achievement. Early reports are already linking the improved atmosphere to increased attendance, circulation, and even improved self-esteem for children where the libraries have already opened (Lau, 2002).

Divergent Perspectives

Modern school library media centers cost millions of dollars. In order to get the maximum use of these facilities, as well as encourage access by students, a variety of what may be considered controversial methods are being employed. Extending the hours the school library media center is open, implementing year-round schools, building combined school-public libraries, and replicating the atmosphere of modern-day bookstores are all being experimented with throughout the United States. Homeschoolers' use of the school library facilities is also a mounting issue. Aside from the impact on the facility itself, concerns related to staffing and the core question of "What is the purpose of the school library?" raise their heads when what might be considered non-traditional uses of the school library media center are discussed.

■ Are School Library Media Centers Necessary?

There is no doubt that school library media centers, if managed correctly, are expensive enterprises. Staff, space, and resources can encompass a significant portion of a school's budget so the pressure is constantly on to prove the worth of the school library media program. This theme, universal and ongoing, is also addressed in the chapters on Virtual School Libraries, Staffing, and Collection Development. In fact, questions from administrators, parents, the public, and even other teachers concerning the necessity of school library media centers are prevalent enough that the Educational Media Association of New Jersey, (EMAnj) publishes *What Do You Say When…: Talking Points: Suggested Responses for Frequently Asked Questions* for members (EMAnj, 2002). Approximately half of the questions are related to facilities:

> ▶ **Question:** Why do we need a school library? Why not distribute library books and magazines to classrooms?
> **Summary of answer:** Concentrating access permits the entire school to equitably, efficiently, and economically

access these resources. The library media specialist is available to teach students how to locate, access, evaluate, and use the information they need.

▶ **Question:** Why do we need a school library? Why can't students go to the public library?
Summary of answer: School library media specialists have knowledge of teaching methods, curriculum, and child development. Not all students have the means to get to a public library, but they all get to school.

▶ **Question:** Why do we need a school library? Why can't students just use the Internet?
Summary of answer: Information in books, magazines, computer software, etc. is distributed by a reputable publisher and has undergone an intensive review process and information on the Internet has not. The school library media specialist gives students the tools to evaluate materials.

Other related facilities questions in the Talking Points (EMAnj, 2002) include extending hours of the school library media center, allowing use by the public, and combining school and public libraries—topics also discussed in this chapter.

■ Extended Hours

The easiest method of getting more use out of library media center facilities is to simply extend the hours it is open. Extended hours refers to hours that the school library media center is open before and after the regular school day, on evenings and weekends, and during the summer. Benefits of extended hours include (Despines, 2001):

▶ The school library media center may be the only library some students can access;
▶ Students have added access to the library, computers, and printers;
▶ The publicity creates community goodwill for the media center and the school;
▶ The opportunity for links from school to home and the community are created;
▶ Areas of the collection not directly related to academic research assignments are used more during extended hours;

- ▶ Parents can help their children with homework within the school setting;
- ▶ The library media center gains status as a community center where students can meet after school;
- ▶ There is time for special programs that are hard to fit into the daily school schedule; and
- ▶ Studies (Lance, et. al, 2000; Krashen, 1999) show that increased time spent in school library media centers increases student achievement and literacy.

Despite the benefits of extended hours listed above, the majority of school library media centers do not offer them. The central issue is staffing. Because a single professional staffs most school libraries, it may only be possible to offer extended hours if that person is agreeable to the practice. Sometimes, teaching contracts place constraints on working extra hours. In schools where there is more than one professional school library media specialist, they have been successful by employing schedules where one person starts earlier in the day and the other stays later while still adhering to a contractually equal number of overall hours.

Other extended hours programs use parent volunteers, library aides, and classroom teachers for staffing. However, this practice assumes that employees not trained as school library media specialists can perform professional duties. For example, one school library media specialist warns that extended hours in her district was a way to use volunteers to "run" the school library media center. "Ambiguity about the unique role of the school library media specialist is dangerous; you should be clear about the precedents you set in your community and school" (Despines, 2001, p. 25).

Closely related to staffing is budgeting for the added salaries that may be required for extended hours. In a well-planned program, schools can incorporate this into their regular budget using the hourly rate in the teaching contract. Other solutions are grants and lobbying the state legislature for funds — a practice that was successful in Florida (Glick, 1998).

Additional reasons cited against extended hours are security concerns, overlap with the public library's hours, and justification of use (Despines, 2001). If you are considering an extended hours program, careful planning is needed and guidance is offered in the Despines (2001) article.

■ Combined School-Public Libraries

One distinctive use of school library facilities is actually a combination of the school and public library in one physical space. These unique libraries can be referred to as combined school-public libraries, joint-use libraries, or shared libraries. Often combining libraries is seen as a cost-saving measure—particularly for rural communities.

Because of the rarity of combined school-public libraries, it is advantageous to understand the pros and cons from the experience of library administrators working in these joint-use facilities. Sager (1999) solicited responses from four such personnel who identified themselves as the public library directors of the shared facilities.

PROS
- ▶ The anticipated intellectual freedom issues have not materialized so far.
- ▶ The shared facility is a high school library during the day following the school district's policies. It is a public library after school and on Saturdays.
- ▶ The community feels its tax dollars are being used wisely.
- ▶ Parents appreciate being able to visit the library while their children are involved in after-school activities.
- ▶ The public library staff has access to teenagers, a hard-to-reach group.
- ▶ Student access to a larger materials collection could be achieved.
- ▶ The public has access to curriculum materials.
- ▶ Student access is available on evenings and weekends.
- ▶ Multiple staff members allows for more service orientation.

CONS
- ▶ Location is a critical component—few members of the general public want to walk down long hallways.
- ▶ The lively school environment can be intimidating to senior citizens and families with young children.
- ▶ Some public library patrons may be a challenge to school security measures.
- ▶ Public use is much smaller compared to similar public libraries.
- ▶ The library is run by the city and the school librarians express distrust.

- ▶ The school librarians have longer summer vacations, more holidays, and shorter workdays but earn more than the public librarians who work year-round. This causes antagonism among staff.
- ▶ Insufficient parking.
- ▶ No money is really saved because the same number of staff is needed and the use of one physical plant is extended.
- ▶ The missions and collection development of both libraries are different (Sager, 1999, pp. 355–358).

The majority of studies on the topic of combined school-public libraries conclude that in order for them to succeed, careful planning is needed. Those considering the feasibility of a joint-use facility will benefit by examining the guidelines published by the Wisconsin Department of Public Instruction (1998). The Department, in response to frequent requests for information on the subject, has compiled a list of issues about combined school-public libraries identified by various studies:

1. School district boundaries and city or village boundaries are usually not identical. This fact raises questions about who is eligible to use the library and how much support each entity is expected to provide.
2. Salaries are usually much higher for school librarians.
3. Certification differs for school and public librarians, with a master's degree (or the equivalent) and a teaching license required of the school librarian, while the qualifications for public librarian certification vary depending on population.
4. The mission of the school library is to support teaching and learning for school age children; the mission of the public library is to meet the information needs of all members of the community. In practice, many public libraries in small communities place a high priority on children and adult recreational reading. The collection(s) must take both missions into consideration.
5. Libraries generally allow unrestricted access to all available materials for all age groups. However, policies of school and public libraries related to access to materials may be significantly different and would need to be reconciled. Public library materials are selected to appeal to a wide range of

interests and ages. The materials in school library collections are carefully selected to match the curriculum and the learning needs and maturity level of the students they serve.

6. Two separate governing agents are required for a combined library. A legally constituted public library requires a board of trustees separate from the school board. All decisions regarding policies and operation affect both school and public service aspects. Consequently,
   - board members must be aware of how decisions will affect both user groups and both administrative structures;
   - boards or their representatives must meet together regularly; and
   - when staff is shared, the two boards or their administrators will occasionally have conflicting opinions about priorities and responsibilities.

7. As with any enterprise, success depends on the perceptions, attitudes, and reactions of potential users. Some adults may not be comfortable in the presence of teenagers or in an environment that favors them. Students may not be eager to return to school after hours, and students from another school might be uncomfortable in a school building other than "their" school.

8. Ideal locations for school and public libraries conflict. A public library should be in the most active area of the community, near businesses, and easily entered with adequate parking adjacent; whereas the school library media center should be as close as possible to classrooms, and the school should be away from the busiest area of the community.

9. Public libraries often receive substantial private donations for a new building or an addition, for starting a new service, or for upgrading an existing collection. Donors may or may not be as likely to give to a public library that is seen as part of a school district.

10. The environments of school and public libraries differ, with the school requiring guidance and group supervision, and the public library emphasizing independence and patron privacy. Activities such as instruction for students, conversation, and special programs for adults may conflict.

11. Easy access for adults sometimes causes a security problem for schools or a concern for children's safety.
12. The cost of a combined library is not so small as the sharing of space and facilities would make it seem. For example, adults or preschoolers and school children usually want to use the library at the same time, rather than at different and complementary times. This affects the total space needed as well as staff, furniture, equipment, and resources. In addition, a public library needs to be open on evenings and weekends and during vacation periods.
13. Daily policy or procedural decisions can be a source of conflict. Will the English class use all the terminals, or will some be reserved for adults?
14. Conflicts are bound to arise over priorities given to the many aspects of library service. Examples include content of the collection, hours of operation, programming, space, and access to such things as seating, equipment, resources, the public catalog, and reference service.
15. In the event of the dissolution of the combination and the establishment of separate libraries, decisions will have to be made as to how to divide the various components (collection, furniture, equipment, software, etc.) (p. 4).

■ The School Library Media Center in Year-Round Schools

There are implications for school library media center facilities in year-round schools. Year-round students attend the same number of days as their traditional counterparts except that these days are arranged differently. A few year-round schools have all their students on the same instructional and vacation schedule (a single-track calendar). Most, however, operate on a multi-track calendar, which groups students onto tracks that have different instructional and vacation schedules. These tracks are stepped so that there is always at least one track on vacation (Ballinger, 1987). The multi-track model allows for the school to be used full-time year-round, allowing for up to 25% more students to attend. However, the school library media center would never have any "down time."

In the summer of 2002, students in this author's course at the University of Hawaii conducted three case studies on the impact of year-round schools on school library media centers in Hawaii, where year-round schooling is commonplace (Simon & Atalig, 2002). Interviews were carried out with school library media specialists at an elementary, a middle, and a high school employing both single and multi-track schedules. The school library media specialists cited the following advantages and disadvantages:

ADVANTAGES
- ▶ School library media specialists in multi-track schools have the opportunity to work a 12-month schedule and earn 25% more salary.
- ▶ School library media specialists in a single-track school (working 45 days on and 15 days off) enjoy the frequent breaks and come back refreshed.
- ▶ Students are studying different units at different times — less demand on the collection.
- ▶ Ordering can be done year-round.
- ▶ Resources are being used to their full capacity.

DISADVANTAGES
- ▶ No down time when working 12 months — leads to burnout.
- ▶ More students in the school demand more of the collection and often the budget is not increased to compensate.
- ▶ No time to do inventory.
- ▶ Keeping in touch with all the teachers who are on different tracks.
- ▶ Challenge in servicing all students on all tracks.
- ▶ Additional duties.
- ▶ Keeping track of circulation and getting materials back.

To gain a better understanding of year-round schools, a good starting point is the Web site of the Heartland Area Education Agency (2003) where there are links to research and news articles. Because little has been written about year-round schools and school library media centers, those considering implementing this schedule would benefit by seeking out other school library media specialist who are currently involved.

■ School Library Media Centers Incorporating Design Ideas from Bookstores

The $2.5 million Homestead High School library in Cupertino, California, is a light and spacious facility with mission-style furniture and plenty of computer terminals. The *San Jose Mercury News* (Corcoran, 2002) reported on other new and renovated school library facilities in California that have wired conference rooms, shelves of new materials, study tables, and even lounging areas and outdoor tables giving them the "enticing air of a Barnes and Noble."

> Critics—including some students who use them—question the need for such amenities, but librarians say it's part of the evolving vision of the school library. "Libraries are becoming places where students go because they like the environment," said Nancy Rowell, school library service coordinator in the San Mateo County Office of Education. "If you want to motivate kids to read, there's nothing better than motivating them to come into the library. We do a little marketing in the way we design libraries these days." (Corcoran, 2002, p.8).

Increasingly, all types of libraries are incorporating design ideas from bookstores in order to lure patrons into the facility and away from the computer terminal located at home, classroom, or dorm room. The trend may have developed out of an *American Libraries* article, "What If You Ran Your Library Like a Bookstore?" Author Steve Coffman (1998) argued that customers flock to bookstores because of an ambiance that encourages patrons to linger, lots of new books, coffee bars, and convenient hours. "If comfortable chairs alone aren't enough of a lure, bookstores now offer a calendar of book talks, book signings, discussion groups, demonstrations, and performances unrivaled by all but the largest urban libraries. They have even started imitating the most sacrosanct of all public library services: story time and summer reading programs" (p. 42).

Editors later remarked, "Judging from the intensity of the letters *American Libraries* received in response to Steve Coffman's "What If You Ran Your Library Like a Bookstore?" the article has provoked an animated debate on a central issue in librarianship: What does a library do and who is it for? (Bookstore Backlash: Wow, Did We Get Letters!,

1998, p. 76). Some points made by letter-writers were that bookstore staff is paid low wages, morale is low and turnover high, bookstore clerks can't answer reference questions, and there is no cataloging of materials for easy access.

Charli O'Dell (1999) is one school library media specialist who has incorporated the bookstore's marketing techniques into her school library media program. O'Dell planned a "Latte Day" where volunteer parents prepared cappuccino, hot chocolate, and hot cider and served it to students while wearing coffee shop aprons. Library chairs were removed to encourage people to circulate, Mozart CDs were played, and 400 new books were on display. O'Dell boasts:

> At the end of the day, we realized we'd sold 1,100 drinks, for a profit of nearly $700! We used some of the money to buy new recycling containers for the school and put the rest in our book account. Luckily my pre-Latte Day fears never materialized. For instance, even though we provided hot cider and hot chocolate, I'd worried that parents might object to their kids drinking coffee at school. But there were no complaints. (I later learned that Swiss Miss cappuccino contains less than half the caffeine found in a can of Coke.) I'd also feared that the media center would be marred by litter and spills. But everything stayed perfectly neat. In fact, the cups became status symbols—icons for maturity, intellectualism, and respect—and the students carried them around all day (p. 35).

■ Homeschoolers

Another area where use of the facilities can potentially become controversial is use by homeschooled children and their parents. Nothing was located in the literature about homeschooling from a school library perspective, but as the numbers of homeschooled children continue to rise, it is predicted that school libraries (particularly those in very rural areas) may be called upon to supply some of the services that public libraries currently provide. As tax-paying citizens of a school district, homeschoolers (children and parents) are entitled to use of the school's facilities. However, there may be policies in place as to when this access is provided. Typically, when members of the general public want to use the school library, an appointment is necessary.

People choose homeschooling for the following reasons (Madden, 1991):

- ▶ Religion/philosophy;
- ▶ To avoid peer-pressure;
- ▶ Greater parent-child contact;
- ▶ To develop better self-concept;
- ▶ To avoid peer competition;
- ▶ To accomplish more academically;
- ▶ To personalize learning; and
- ▶ Because of poor local schools (economically and educationally).

Many of the reasons people give for homeschooling their children may give rise to feelings of resentment of the homeschooling parents and their children by the school library staff and other teachers. The attitude is, "If we aren't good enough to educate your child, why should we let them have the benefit of the school's resources?" "Staff Bias Against Homeschoolers" is the focus of a chapter in *The Librarian's Guide to Homeschooling Resources* (Scheps, 1998), one of the few books on the issue. Suggested solutions are sensitivity training sessions especially led in tandem with local homeschoolers, and proof of well-adjusted and comfortable kids as examples. Other chapters deal with potential problems in serving homeschoolers such as censorship attempts and heavy use of interlibrary loan.

The vast majority of the literature on libraries and homeschooling focuses on public libraries. Some of the concerns facing public libraries could potentially develop in schools such as subject wipe-out—families taking out everything available on a topic—time and energy demands on staff, technology demands, and inability to cater to homeschoolers' exclusive needs (Madden, 1991).

In an attempt to gather data about homeschoolers' use of school libraries, this author posted a survey to a homeschool listserv. Only a few responses were obtained, with all of them responding that they had exclusively used excellent public libraries. One homeschooling parent mentioned about interlibrary loan services and the discussion took off on that tangent. On the school library listserv, LM_NET, homeschooling was only mentioned in reference to problems with homeschoolers returning books and giving discarded materials to homeschoolers.

■ Furnishings

Aside from the facility itself, several quandaries may arise regarding the furnishings within the school library media center. More often than not, these problems occur when a new school library facility is built. Some examples are:

- ▶ Funding runs out and there isn't money to buy any furnishings so tables and chairs from the "old" library are used.
- ▶ The school library media specialist is bypassed in the selection of the furnishings and inappropriate choices are made. This author had first-hand experience working in a school library where an administrator thought it would be more prestigious to enlist the help of a local academic librarian to choose the furnishings for the new prep school library. She selected study carrels exclusively (perhaps appropriate for an academic library, but not a high school) which made it impossible to monitor the floor and for students to work in small groups.
- ▶ In an attempt to present the school library as a "showplace," trendy or gaudy furnishings are chosen which go out of style quickly.

Another issue of concern is that as technology infiltrates existing school library media centers, getting more computers may take precedence over buying ergonomic desks and chairs. Often new equipment is simply placed on existing tables and desks, without regard for any physical repercussions this practice may have on students who spend countless hours in front of a computer screen either slumped or craning their necks. An ergonomically designed workstation for children will incorporate the following features:

- ▶ Students' feet are on the floor.
- ▶ Students are looking down, not up, at the screen.
- ▶ Students can hold their arms at a 90-degree angle as they use keyboards.
- ▶ Keyboards are resting on keyboard shelves below the level of the standard desk or tabletop (Minkel, 2001).

Careful planning will prevent money from becoming an obstacle in the purchase of furniture. A comprehensive master plan should include the costs of furniture and other equipment that could be incorporated into a school's capital spending requests or bond proposals (Kennedy, 2000). Also, by planning and choosing furniture that is durable and takes maximum advantage of available space, it will result in fewer pieces of furniture needing replacement and you will need to persuade officials to squeeze money from a tight budget less often (Kennedy, 2000). Developing a plan, and sharing it with administrators, may possibly prevent some of the aforementioned furnishing dilemmas.

And finally, color holds subtle messages. On one visit to a school library intern, my student remarked that the boys at her middle school site, where the library's walls and countertops were pink, referred to it as the "girls' library." In a profession that is predominantly female, one must make efforts to create an environment where both boys and girls, as well as all ethnic groups, will feel welcomed and at ease. Beyond color, accents such as posters, plants, objects, displays, and bulletin boards should incorporate this effort.

An effective and inviting school library media center is often referred to as the "hub of the school." When students feel comfortable in this hub, they can potentially learn and work better. School library media centers today are pushing design, programming, and access boundaries to attract and accommodate students' needs in the information age.

Questions for Discussion and Reflection

1. Describe the best school library media center facility you have ever visited.

2. What is your reaction to Charli O'Dell's "Latte Day?" Do you think this is something that could work on a regular basis in a school library media center?

3. How can school libraries compete with bookstores? Do you think they should have to or not?

4. What might a school library facility look like 20 years from now?

5. What are some things you might be able to accomplish with your school library media program in a year-round school that you couldn't in a traditional school and vice versa?

Projects

1. Interview a parent and child involved in homeschooling about their use of libraries.

2. Use some of the resources listed in Additional Information to develop a survey for students that gathers their opinions about how they would like the school library media center to look and feel and when they would like it to be open. Give the survey to a cross-section of students in a school and report on your findings.

3. Determine which is the best school library media center facility in your immediate area. Arrange to spend at least one full day there and observe the impact of the surroundings on students and teachers. Make a presentation on your findings.

References

Ballinger, C.E. (1987). *The year-round school: where learning never stops*. Bloomington, Indiana: Phi Delta Kappa Educational Foundation, 1987.

Bookstore backlash: Wow, did we get letters! (1998, May). *American Libraries, 29* (5), 76–79.

Cocoran, K. (2002, Jun. 1). Public school libraries back in circulation: State push revives abandoned programs. *San Jose Mercury News*, 8.

Coffman, S. (1998, March). What if you ran your library like a bookstore? *American Libraries, 29* (3), 40–44.

Despines, J. (2001, Nov./Dec.). Planning for extended hours. *Knowledge Quest, 30* (2), 22–26.

DeWitt-Wallace Reader's Digest Fund (1999). *Executive summary: Findings from the evaluation of the national library power program*. Retrieved July 8, 2003 from <www.wallacefunds.org/frames/framesetpublications.htm>.

EMAnj (2002). *EMAnj talking points toolkit*. Educational Media Association of New Jersey: Authors.

Glick, A. (1998, May). School's out at 3, but Florida's media centers stay open. *School Library Journal, 44* (5), 16.

Heartland Area Education Agency (2003). *Year-round education*. Retrieved July 8, 2003, from <www.aea11.k12.ia/us/curriculum/yre.html>.

Kennedy, M. (2000, October). Connected and comfortable. *American School & University, 73* (2), 35–38.

Krashen, S. (1993). *The power of reading: Insights from the research*. Englewood, CO: Libraries Unlimited.

Lance, K.C. (2001). *LRS school library media impact studies*. Retrieved July 8, 2003, from <www.lrs.org/html/about/school_studies.html>.

Lau, D. (2002, Mar.). The shape of tomorrow. *School Library Journal, 48* (3), 57–60.

Madden, S.B. (1991, July). Learning at home. *School Library Journal, 37* (7), 23–25.

Minkel, W. (2001, Mar.). Kids, computers, and comfort. *School Library Journal, 47* (3), 33.

O'Dell, C. (1999, Dec.). Thanks a-latte. *School Library Journal, 45* (12), 35–36.

Sager, D., Myers, C., Register, J., Johns, M. & Kleiman, A.M. (1999). Changing perspectives: Joint use of facilities by schools and public libraries. *Public Libraries, 38* (6), 355–359.

Scheps, S.G. (1998). *The librarian's guide to homeschooling resources.* Chicago: American Library Association.

Simon, J. & Atalig, K. (2002). *Year-round scheduling in Hawaii's school libraries.* Unpublished raw data.

Wisconsin Department of Public Instruction (1998). *Combined school and public libraries: guidelines for decision-makers.* 2nd ed. Madison, WI: Division for Libraries, Technology, and Community Learning, Wisconsin Department of Public Instruction.

Additional Information

Baule, S.M. (1999). *Facilities planning for school library media and technology centers.* Worthington, OH: Linworth Publishing, Inc.

Erikson, R. & Markuson, C. (2001). *Designing a school library media center for the future.* Chicago: American Library Association.

Everhart, N.L. (1998). "Facilities" in *Evaluating the school library media center: Analysis techniques and research practices.* Englewood, CO: Libraries Unlimited.

Hughes-Hassell, S. & Wheelock, A. (2001). "Refurbishing for Learning" in *The information-powered school.* Chicago: American Library Association.

Scargall, H. (1999, Nov./Dec.). Color in architecture. *Library Talk, 12* (5), 11–12.

Taney, K.B. (2002). *Teen Spaces: The step-by-step library makeover.* Chicago, IL: American Library Association.

Walters, D. (2001, May/June). Media center makeovers. *The Book Report, 20* (1), 54–55.

Web Sites

Combined Libraries: A Bibliography
    <www.ala.org/library/fact20.html>
    Compiled by the American Library Association, there are links to select articles and books on the subject of combined libraries.

Cornell University Human Factors and Ergonomics Laboratory
    <ergo.human.cornell.edu/MBergo/intro.html>
    Provides analysis of child computer use and ergonomic abuse.

Library Media Centers: National Clearinghouse for Educational Facilities
    <www.edfacilities.org/rl/libraries.cfm>
    A resource list of links, books, and journal articles on the design of K–12 school libraries.

Reflections on the 'New' Bookstores
    <www.trelease-on-reading.com/whatsnu_4.html>
    Taken from Jim Trelease's online version of *The Read-Aloud Handbook*, this chapter presents arguments for incorporating ideas from bookstores into schools and school libraries.

Welcome to the Coffee Cup: Cafes & Libraries
    <www.librarysupportstaff.com/coffeelibs.html>
    Links to full-text articles in newspapers describing successful libraries/cafes around the country.

Virtual/Digital School Libraries

What is a virtual school library? According to the Online Dictionary of Library and Information Science (ODLIS):

> A virtual library is a "library without walls" in which the collections do not exist on paper, microform, or in any tangible form, but are accessible in digital format. Such libraries exist only on a very small scale, but in many traditional libraries, catalogs and indexes are available online, and the full-text of some periodicals and reference works is also available electronically. Some libraries and library systems call themselves "virtual" because they offer online services (example: Colorado Virtual Library). The term digital library is more appropriate because the term virtual (borrowed from "virtual reality") suggests that the experience of using such a library is not the same as the "real" thing, when in fact, the experience of reading or viewing a document on a computer screen may be qualitatively different from reading the same publication in print, but the information content is the same regardless of format" (Reitz, 2002).

For the purposes of discussion in this chapter, virtual and digital libraries will be referred to interchangeably. School libraries offering online services beyond their library walls will also be considered virtual libraries.

Divergent Perspectives

Virtual school libraries present a number of challenges for school library media specialists. As virtual school libraries evolve, roles of school library media specialists are being redefined. Who accesses virtual school libraries, along with when and where, present copious concerns. Digital libraries, provided by state departments of education and state libraries, and electronic books are two technologies impacting school library media center programs. Measuring the use of digital libraries takes on increased importance as the use of print resources declines.

■ Roles of the Virtual School Library and Virtual School Librarian

Virtual libraries, and more specifically virtual school libraries, have a relatively short history that began in the mid 1990s. A review of the literature shows an evolution of thought about virtual school libraries commencing with debating their value and significance, up to the present dialogue on how to manage them. Most virtual, or digital, school libraries conform to the portion of the ODLIS definition in that they consider themselves digital because they offer online services.

No current statistics are available about the number of schools that have virtual school libraries, or even school library Web pages. Peter Milbury's *Network of School Librarian Web Pages* (2002), a collection of Web pages created or maintained by school librarians, links to over 1,000 sites but is not considered to be comprehensive. Some of the best school library Web sites have been awarded the International Association of School Librarianship's (IASL) Concord School Library Web Page Award (IASL, 2002). There are monthly and yearly awards.

The 2001 annual winner of the IASL award, one of the most comprehensive virtual school libraries on the web, is the Springfield Township High School Virtual Library in Pennsylvania managed by school library media specialist Joyce Valenza (2002). It includes information about the school, library staff, links to resources for teachers, links to resources for students, a reference desk, a college and career center, and an MLA style sheet. Literally hundreds of links are arranged according to subjects being taught in classes. Another example is the "invisible library" created by Kathy Lehman (2002) at the Thomas Dale High School in Chesterfield, Virginia. Because her school library was closed for months for remodeling, Lehman used the time the physical library was closed to create the "invisible library." She set up links to subscription databases and other local libraries, trained faculty and students, and developed class lists — Web pages designed collaboratively with teachers to guide students through specific classroom research objectives. Pleased with the outcome, Lehman observed:

> Clearly students recognize the value of edited, authoritative material. Teachers remarked that students were more focused when using the class Web pages. One science teacher observed that students with attention problems who have trouble in other class activities stayed on task when directed from the class Web page. Everyone is equally engaged at the same time. One student summed up an overwhelming benefit of directed Internet access by commenting that "more students can be looking at the same thing and not have to wait around on a book." (Lehman, 2002, p. 29).

Both Joyce Valenza and Kathy Lehman are working hard to redirect the penchant students have for Internet surfing to that of using more authoritative electronic sources via their virtual libraries. This may be easier said than done. According to the 2000 report from the Pew Research Center titled "Internet and American Life," it was revealed:

> For many teens, the Internet has replaced the library as the primary tool for doing research for significant projects. Almost all teens with access to the Internet use it to do research for school — 94% report using the Internet for this purpose. "I find the Internet most useful when I need help for school," maintained a 15-year-old boy who answered questions in an online discussion group run by the research firm Greenfield Online for the Pew Internet Project. "Without the Internet you need to go to the library and walk around looking for books. In today's world you can just go home and get into the Internet and type in your search term. The results are endless. There is so much information that you have to ignore a lot of it."
>
> When asked to think about the last big report they wrote for school, 71% of online teens reported relying mostly

on Internet sources for their research. Another quarter (24%) reported using mostly library sources, and 4% said they used both equally. Older teens were slightly more likely than younger ones to report relying on Internet sources; 74% of those ages 15–17 relied on the Internet for their most recent project, compared to 68% of those ages 12–14. And three-quarters of youths who go online every day used the Internet as their main source for their last school report, compared to 68% of youths who go online less often. Students cite the ease and speed of online research as their main reasons for relying on the Web instead of the library (Lenhart, 2002).

The Pew finding, that the Internet has replaced the library for teens, is a foremost concern for school librarians. In December 2001, e-global library, a division of Jones Knowledge,™ Inc., commissioned a survey entitled "The Role of the Librarian in the Digital Age" (E-global library, 2001). When school librarians were asked, "What do you think are the most significant challenges facing librarians today?" 90% responded: "The perception that everything can be found on the Internet." The same group of school librarians expect their digital responsibilities to increase. The highest percentage (32%) said they answered 41–50% of their reference questions using the Internet, and 44% expect to be answering more than 70% of their reference questions using the Internet two years from now. Table 1 lists the areas that librarians wish they had learned more about during their studies.

Table 1: Areas librarians wish they had learned more about in their studies.

Web content creation and design	61%
electronic or virtual reference	59%
systems technology	55%
online research	43%
providing online services to online learners	34%

School library media specialists are at a crossroads. They realize they must redefine themselves to manage the technology and to make it available efficiently and effectively. They must fight the perception that "everything can be found on the Internet" in order to preserve their jobs in states where school librarians aren't mandated. School library media specialists are needed more than ever to integrate the information technologies into the curriculum, teach information literacy, and direct students and teachers to the best quality resources.

■ Accessing the Virtual School Library

"Electronic information services, and networks provided directly or indirectly by the library, should be equally, readily, and equitably accessible to all library users" (AASL/AECT, 1998, p. 164). Providing equitable access to a school virtual library will be difficult if the goal of the library is that resources will be accessible to students from home. A gap exists between students who have access to information technology and those who don't. The term "digital divide" is used to describe this gap between those who can effectively use new information and communication tools, such as the Internet, and those who cannot.

The report, "Inside the Digital Divide: Connecting Youth to Opportunities in the New Economy," (Pearlman, 2002) states that 75% of America's poorest households were still not online in late 2001, compared to only 20% in homes earning over $75,000 per year. Hispanics (31.8%) and African Americans (39.8%) lag significantly behind whites (59%) in Internet access at home. There is also a growing divide in high-speed broadband connections. Almost twice as many urban households were connected to the Internet via high-speed broadband Internet access (21.2%) as their rural counterparts (12.2%).

Access to virtual school libraries is also frequently provided to students throughout the school campus — in classrooms and computer labs. There are advantages to this arrangement: information needs can be met immediately, and use of the library is extended, especially when libraries are small with limited seating. School library media specialists in these schools must make a concerted effort to connect with classroom teachers to ensure that students have skills in accessing and evaluating the information available to make maximum use of this access. When extending access of licensed databases beyond the school library media center, additional fees will apply.

■ 24–7 Access

Many school library Web sites serving as a virtual library include a link on the site where the school librarian can be e-mailed and asked questions. Is the school library media specialist now obligated to provide 24-hour service? What about weekends and holidays? Does the school library media specialist receive overtime pay? Do students who have home computers receive special services that other students do not? These, and other, questions will have to be addressed as information technology grows and more students gain access from home.

The current literature on 24–7 reference is directed exclusively to public and academic libraries, not schools. These libraries are grappling with the issue and solutions include: the librarians manning different shifts, answering questions only during certain times, and outsourcing other tasks—unsatisfactory options for most school libraries. In northeast Ohio, a suitable arrangement has been that a consortium of fourteen public libraries provides live chat and voice via the Internet from 8 p.m. until midnight. Area students can chat with professional librarians and get professional help with their homework and other research and reference questions. One school librarian works one night a week from her home PC for askusquestions.com (2002). An alternative to manning a virtual reference desk is to link to your local public library's virtual reference desk. If there isn't one, The Virtual Reference Desk Learning Center for Kids sponsored by the United States Department of Education (2002) and manned by volunteer librarians, allows students to ask reference questions.

■ State Digital Libraries

An increasing number of state libraries have taken the initiative to provide digital libraries for the residents of their state, which obviously includes students (Berkeley Digital Library SunSITE, 2002). Connecticut even has *The Connecticut Digital Library Resources for Schools* (2002) incorporating licensed databases, access to online catalogs throughout the state, and preselected links arranged by subject. The goals of iCONN, a typical state digital library, is to:

▶ ensure universal access to a core level of library and information resources for every resident of Connecticut through their public library, school, college, and from home;

- help provide necessary information resources to every school in Connecticut so that all students are prepared to function in an information society;
- provide information resources to the increasing number of students taking advantage of online courses at Connecticut's colleges and universities;
- enhance the quality of teaching, research and education at Connecticut's colleges and universities by supporting online information resources; and
- support the information needs of all Connecticut citizens (The Connecticut Digital Library Resources for Schools, 2002).

State digital libraries offer considerable advantages to schools. The most obvious is the tremendous cost savings for subscription databases. They are provided free or at a much-reduced fee to participating schools. Another advantage is from the educational perspective. Students are exposed to a consistent set of information tools throughout their schooling and beyond. They can more easily make transitions between schools, grade levels, and lifelong learning. Library media specialists may be offered professional development opportunities and educational support materials through the state library.

■ The Internet Is No Substitute for a Library

One key drawback of state digital libraries, and the Internet in general, has been that they have provided the impetus for school administrators to decrease school library media staff and budgets. Feeling that computers and connectivity to electronic resources are enough to do the job, principals see the school librarian and books as expendable.

Mark Herring (2001) in "10 Reasons the Internet Is No Substitute for a Library" makes some solid arguments on the other side. Herring argues:

> The Web is great; but it's a woefully poor substitute for a full-service library. It is mad idolatry to make it more than a tool. Libraries are icons of our cultural intellect, totems to the totality of knowledge. If we make them obsolete, we've signed the death warrant to our collective national conscience, not to mention sentencing what's left of our culture to the waste bin

of history. No one knows better than librarians just how much it costs to run a library. We're always looking for ways to trim expenses while not contracting service. The Internet is marvelous, but to claim, as some now do, that it's making libraries obsolete is as silly as saying shoes have made feet unnecessary (Herring, 2001, p. 76).

His 10 reasons are:

1. Not everything is on the Internet.
2. The needle (your search) in the haystack (the Web).
3. Quality control doesn't exist.
4. What you don't know really does hurt you.
5. States can now buy one book and distribute it to every library on the Web — NOT!
6. Hey, Bud, you forgot about eBook readers.
7. Aren't there library-less universities now?
8. But a virtual state library would do it, right?
9. The Internet: A mile wide, an inch (or less) deep.
10. The Internet is ubiquitous, but books are portable.

■ eBooks

Most virtual school libraries are providing links to nonfiction resources, both pay and free, related to the curriculum. Fiction books are often neglected. Access to fiction books, as well as textbooks, can be supplied by means of eBooks, or electronic books. eBooks are digital copies of books that can be accessed via virtual libraries, online booksellers, library jobbers, publishers, and other sites.

eBooks have both advantages and disadvantages.

ADVANTAGES
- ▶ eBooks are cheaper — they are less than half the price of regular books;
- ▶ eBooks have search, annotation, and dictionary features that printed books do not have;
- ▶ different languages are available for the same book;

- ► font size can be adjusted;
- ► backlight allows one to read at night;
- ► many textbooks can be downloaded to a compact reader; no more 40-pound backpacks; and
- ► eBooks can be accessed from anywhere and downloaded in minutes.

DISADVANTAGES
- ► no browsing ability like in a traditional library or bookstore;
- ► people have emotional ties to their favorite printed books;
- ► not having the physical feel and look of books or being able to judge a book's popularity by how worn it is;
- ► Pocket readers are expensive;
- ► need for batteries and electricity; not as transportable as printed books; and
- ► not all books have electronic versions - limited selection for children.

Other advantages and disadvantages of the eBook format are related to the type of device that is employed to read them.

Laptops

ADVANTAGES
- ► power and multifunctionality of a full-fledged computer.

DISADVANTAGES
- ► bulkiness and low-contrast screens for reading, and
- ► one laptop per student is an expensive proposition at approximately $1,000.

Palm OS devices

ADVANTAGES
- ► least expensive option-ranging from $150–$300, and
- ► offer a growing amount of third-party educational applications in addition to eBook capabilities.

DISADVANTAGES
▶ small screen size and low resolutions—conditions not ideal for reading longer works.

Pocket PCs

ADVANTAGES
▶ priced in the middle of laptops and Palm OS devices at around $450, and
▶ have higher screen resolutions than the Palm OS devices and come with some of the reader software built-in.

Dedicated eBook readers

ADVANTAGES
▶ ergonomically designed for reading;
▶ can be carried around easily like a book;
▶ offer good screen resolutions; and
▶ are more cost-effective than laptops.

DISADVANTAGES
▶ dedicated to one use.

Many of the problems with eBooks are being addressed as technology advances. Major vendors such as Baker and Taylor and Follett are now offering eBook catalogs as well as eBooks in Adobe PDF format. A wide variety of titles is available including those for children and young adults. According to recent Adobe sales literature (Adobe, 2003) eBooks improve and extend access and feature text-to-speech options, Web links, rich graphics and images, enhanced search capabilities, and ever-improving portability. An excellent Web site for librarians interested in incorporating eBooks is "Electronic Books in Libraries" (Gibbons, 2002). There you can locate information on eBook studies, products, and Web sites and sign up for a free bi-monthly newsletter providing information about eBook products, content, and the market specifically for a librarian audience.

■ Measuring Use

As students increase their use of electronic sources in a virtual library environment, measuring the effectiveness of the virtual library in meeting student needs also intensifies. Students will be accessing the virtual library at home and at other sites throughout the school such as classrooms and computer labs. Relying on traditional circulation and attendance figures is ill-advised. These figures will decline in a digital environment, and it will appear as if you are doing a poor job.

To solve this problem, Charles McClure urges, "We have to start counting the right stuff," which according to McClure, is found at least in part in analysis of user connect sessions, document downloads, and Web log records. Instead of dividing library measures into two categories—traditional transactions versus digital ones—McClure advocates that libraries begin doing composite statistics, which blend the two counts: "Web-site visits and turnstile counts should be put together for a composite measure. A visit to the library can be on the Web," he argued (Burek, 2002, p. 45).

Although McClure was addressing public librarians and patrons' use offsite, his suggestions apply to schools as well. Additional measures for on-site use in schools are:

> *Fill Rate*—The fill rate is defined as the percentage of successful searches for materials in any part of the library collection and is calculated by dividing the number of successful searches by all searches. Users need to be interviewed as they leave the library in order to determine the fill rate.
> *OPAC/Network Reports*—Reports can provide details on patron searching and can generate statistics on the number of searches; how many were successful or unsuccessful; and searches matching certain parameters. Software for networked terminals offers additional reports. For example, it is possible to monitor searches per terminal, per location, by the databases used, or by the Web sites accessed. When students are assigned individual passwords, reporting software is capable of generating statistics on individuals as to where, when, what, and how they used network programs.
> *Observation*—Observation will often clarify what automated reporting systems don't reflect. Student behaviors at computer terminals might involve asking others for help, using printed

guides, revealing body language, and verbal comments. When using observation as an evaluation technique, the behavior to be studied must be defined and the process used to observe must be standardized. Designing a data collection form or checklist is imperative.

Examining Student Work—Examining student work may be employed to determine the number, types, and currency of sources; use of other libraries; and the search process itself. Methods for examination include checking bibliographies, assigning logs to keep track of the research process, and developing incremental rubrics to assess information literacy skills (Everhart, 2000, pp. 58–60).

Virtual school libraries and eBooks, phenomena taking a foothold in present and future school libraries, need to be planned for and managed carefully. School library media specialists should monitor the development of virtual libraries and eBooks in both public and academic libraries where they are more commonplace.

Questions for Discussion and Reflection

1. How will maintaining a virtual school library impact on the workload of the school library media specialist? In what areas will his or her workload potentially be increased or decreased?

2. Does your state have a digital library? If so, how is it utilized in schools?

3. What are some other methods that might be employed to measure students' use of electronic resources?

4. What would an ideal virtual school library contain? How would the physical library complement it?

5. Discuss some strategies you could use to bridge the digital divide in your school library media program.

Projects

1. Interview or survey at least 50 teenagers about the resources they use for their research. Write a report of your findings comparing them to the Pew Report.

2. Develop a collaborative unit that encompasses eBooks.

3. Access state virtual libraries from the Berkeley Web site <sunsite.berkeley.edu/Libweb/usa-state.html>. Evaluate them and recommend three that are the most appropriate for school use. Justify your selections.

References

Adobe (2003). *eBook catalog.* Retrieved February 25, 2003 from <ebooks.adobe.com>.

American Association of School Librarians, & Association for Educational Communications and Technology. (1998). *Information power: Building partnerships for learning.* Chicago: American Library Association.

AskUsQuestions.com. (2003). Retrieved July 8, 2003, from <www.askusquestions.com>.

Berkeley Digital Library SunSITE. (2003, July 8). Libraries on the web: USA state. Retrieved July 8, 2003, from <sunsite.berkeley.edu/Libweb/usa-state.html>.

Burek Pierce, J. (2002, May). Digital discomfort? "Get over it," says McClure. *American Libraries, 33* (5), 45.

The Connecticut Digital Library Resources for Schools. (2003). About iCONN. Retrieved July 8, 2003, from Connecticut Education Network Web site at: <www.iconn.org/about.html>.

E-Global Library. (2001). *The role of the librarian in the digital age.* Retrieved September 17, 2002, from <www.egloballibrary.com>.

Everhart, N. (2000, Jan/Feb). Evaluating school library information services in the digital age. *The Book Report, 18* (4), 58–60.

Gibbons, S. (2002). eBooks *Studies: Study challenges.* Retrieved July 18, 2003, from <www.lib.rochester.edu/main/eBooks/studies/challenges.htm>.

Gibbons, S. (2002). Electronic books in libraries. Retrieved July 18, 2003, from <www.lib.rochester.edu/main/eBooks/index.html>.

Herring, M.Y. (2001, April). 10 reasons the Internet is no substitute for a library [Electronic version]. *American Libraries, 32* (4), 76–78.

International Association of School Librarianship. (2003, March 19). *IASL Concord school library web page award.* Retrieved July 8, 2003, from <www.iasl-slo.org/web_award.html>.

Lehman, K. (2002, April). Promoting library advocacy and information literacy from an "Invisible library." *Teacher-Librarian, 29* (4), 27–29.

Lehman, K. (2003, May 14). *Thomas Dale High School library media center*. Retrieved July 8, 2003, from<chesterfield.k12.va.us/Schools/Dale_HS/library/Virtlib/media.htm>.

Lenhart, A., Simon, M., & Graziano, M. (2002). *The Internet and education: Findings of the Pew Internet & American life project.* Retrieved July 8, 2003, from Pew Internet Report at the Pew Web site <www.pewinternet.org/reports/pdfs/PIP_Schools_Report.pdf>.

Milbury, P. (2003, January 12). *Peter Milbury's network of school library web pages*. Retrieved July 8, 2003, from <www.school-libraries.net>.

Pearlman, B. (2002). *Inside the digital divide: Connecting youth to opportunities in the new economy.* Retrieved July 8, 2003, from Digital Divide Network Web site: <www.DigitalDivideNetwork.org/content/stories/index.cfm?key=224>.

Reitz, J.M. (2002). *Online dictionary of library and information science.* Retrieved July 8, 2003, from Western Connecticut State University, Ruth A. Hass Library Web site at: <vax.wcsu.edu/library/odlis.html#V>.

United States Department of Education. (2003) VRD presents The Learning Center. Retrieved July 8, 2003, from <www.askvrd.org/vrd>.

Valenza, J. (2003, June 13). *Springfield Township High School virtual library.* Retrieved July 8, 2003, from <mciunix.mciu.k12.pa.us/~spjvweb>.

Additional Information

Barron, D.D. (2000, April). The digital divide: Can school library media specialists help build the bridge? *School Library Media Activities Monthly, 16* (8), 47–51.

Dresang, E.T. (1999). *Radical change: Books for youth in a digital age.* New York: H.W. Wilson.

Web Sites

The Benton Foundation
    <www.benton.org>
    The mission of the Benton Foundation is to articulate a public interest vision for the digital age and to demonstrate the value of communications for solving social problems. Benton demonstrates and promotes the use of digital media to engage, equip, and connect people to alleviate social ills. Timely research reports are available.

The Berkeley Digital Library SunSITE
    <sunsite.berkeley.edu/>
    SunSITE helps to build digital collections and services while providing information and support to digital library developers worldwide. They are sponsored by The Library, U.C. Berkeley, and Sun Microsystems, Inc.

D-Lib Forum
    <www.dlib.org>
    Resources for those interested in digital libraries and electronic publishing, including the monthly *D-Lib Magazine*, a compilation of contributed stories, commentary and briefings.

Open eBook Forum
    <www.openeBook.org>
    A forum for the discussion of issues and technologies related to electronic books.

Rippel, C. (2001). *What is the role of eBooks in libraries?*
    <skyways.lib.ks.us/central/ebooks/>
    Covers numerous issues such as acquisitions, cataloging, marketing, and circulation of eBooks in libraries.

We Read: Literacy and Education for Life
    <www.weread.org>
    The purpose of this non-profit organization, which utilizes the Internet and technology, is to engage children and young adults in the joys of reading, and raise the awareness of the importance of reading among parents. Free eBooks for kids are available.

Sources of Free eBooks

The Internet Public Library
 <www.ipl.org/reading/books/>
The International Children's Digital Library (ICDL)
 <www.icdlbooks.org>
Electronic Text Center — University of Virginia Library
 <etext.lib.virginia.edu>
Project Gutenberg
 <promo.net/pg/>

Sources for Buying eBooks

NetLibrary
 <www.netllibrary.com>
ChildrensElibrary
 <www.childrenselibrary.com>
Kids@Random
 <www.randomhouse.com/kids/randomview/index.html>

 eBooks are also available at online bookstores such Amazon <www.amazon.com>, Barnes and Noble <www.bn.com>, and Powell's <www.powells.com>.

Glossary

AASL — (American Association of School Librarians) A division of the American Library Association (ALA) serving elementary and secondary school library media specialists and others who provide such services for children and young adults.

Accredited (Accreditation) — A voluntary system of evaluation of higher-education institutions and programs based on self-evaluation and peer-assessment for improvement of academic quality and public accountability. Accreditation assures that higher-education institutions and their units, schools, or programs meet certain pre-existing standards of quality.

Accelerated Reader — Computerized reading management program produced by Renaissance Learning. Students select books from 50,000 titles, take quizzes audibly as well as visually, and the program products individualized report/feedback on the students' progress.

Acquisition — The process of obtaining library materials by purchase, gift, or exchange, often includes a pre-purchase bibliographic searching, selecting, ordering, receiving new materials, processing invoices, and maintaining pertinent documents of transactions.

ALA — (American Library Association) Founded in 1876, the oldest and largest professional library organization representing all types of libraries: state, public, academic and school libraries, special libraries serving government agencies, commerce and industry, the arts, the armed services, hospitals, prisons, and other institutions.

Block scheduling — Scheduling pattern in which a daily class schedule is organized into longer class periods to allow flexibility for instructional activities, usually at the middle and high school levels.

Book Adventure — A free Web-based reading incentive program for students in grade K–8 initially developed and funded by Sylvan Learning Centers and Sylvan Learning Foundation in April of

1999. Students choose books from 6,000 titles currently, subsequently take quizzes on the books they read, and accumulate reward points.

Book talk — A method intended to motivate readers in which librarians or teachers give a glimpse of the book and entice the listener's interest.

Certification — The process by which a state agency or authorized organization evaluates the qualifications of an individual to perform a specific service in return for granting a credential.

Climate — The ambiance or mood that is created from the use of color, decoration, and furnishings within a facility.

Collection development policy — A formal written statement of the principles guiding a library's selection of materials, including criteria used in making selection and weeding decisions as well as acceptance of donations.

Combined school-public library — A facility that houses both a school and a public library in one building. Also known as joint-use library or shared library.

Computerized reading management program — Computer software for self-assessment and management of reading practice. Usually generates multiple-choice questions based on themes and events of books.

Digital divide — The gap in access to information between those who can afford access to computers and those in low-income families and neighborhoods who cannot afford network access.

Digital library — A managed collection of information where the information is stored in digital formats and accessible over a network. The type of original materials can range from books, photographs, serials, and archival materials, audio to "born digital" documents, which are documents without a physical object.

Distance learning — Instruction and learning via communications media (correspondence, television, Internet) with little or no classroom or other face-to-face contact between students and teachers. Students study at their own convenience regardless of time and space.

eBook — Books in a digital form, delivered to the user in machine-readable format onto displays such as a computer monitor or an eBook reader device.

Emergency certificate — A certificate issued to an educator who is teaching out of his or her area of certification which allows him or her to work while simultaneously taking coursework to get certified. Usually issued when no candidates with appropriate certification can be found to fill a position.

Endorsement program — A non-degree program of study preparing certified teachers to add endorsements in additional subject areas to an existing teaching certificate.

Ergonomic — Design that incorporates ease of use, comfort, safety, and efficiency.

Extended hours — Hours a school library media center is open beyond the regular school day — usually before and after school, on weekends, and in the summer.

Extrinsic rewards (Extrinsic motivation) — Motivation or encouragement that comes from an outside force such as money or recognition. Opposite of intrinsic reward.

Fixed scheduling — A library media center schedule based on students coming to the library at the same time each week.

Flexible scheduling — A library media center schedule based on students coming to the school library media center when the need arises in order to meet specific learning objectives. Also called flexible access.

Guidelines — Recommendations from state government education or professional organizations on how to administer a school library media program.

Homeschooling — Education of children at home, usually by a parent.

IASL (International Association of School Librarianship) — a worldwide organization of school library media professionals whose objectives include advocacy for development of school libraries throughout all countries and to foster a sense of community among school librarians in all parts of the world.

Intrinsic rewards (Intrinsic motivation) — Motivation or encouragement that comes from within oneself for enjoyment, satisfaction, desire, or pride of accomplishing a task. Opposite of extrinsic rewards.

Invisible library — Also called virtual library in which access to bibliographic data, full text, images and other information is only accessible electronically.

Joint-use library — *See* combined school-public library.

Library media center — Facility in a school that houses educational resources which can include fiction and nonfiction books, electronic resources, and audiovisual materials, is managed by a school library media specialist, and offers information services to students and teachers.

Library media specialist—A professional staff person who holds a degree with a specialty in school library media and is licensed by the appropriate state agency.

Library Power—National grant program established by the DeWitt Wallace-Reader's Digest Fund in 1988. Grants were offered to restore library services in public elementary and secondary schools, especially in low socio-economic communities and to increase awareness on how school libraries can contribute in the education of the nation's children. To receive grants, schools had to hire and pay salaries for full-time library media specialists, maintain a flexible schedule, and increase spending for books and other materials.

Mandate—A requirement put forth by a governing body; in the case of school library media center programs, it is the state department of education.

M.L.S.—The post-baccalaureate degree of Master of Library Science granted upon completion of a required course of study.

LM_NET—An online discussion group, or listserv, focused on topics of interest to the school library media community. The group is open to school library media specialists and to people involved with library media field to share information, ask for input, and link schools through their school library media center.

Multi-track schedule—A method of scheduling students in year-round schools whereby several groups of students go to school on overlapping blocks of time, or tracks. Usually the school operates on three, four, or five schedules with students having either 60 days in school and 20 days out of school or 45 days in school and 15 days out of school.

NCATE—(National Council for Accreditation of Teacher Education A non-profit, non-governmental organization that accredits undergraduate and graduate teacher education programs.

Paraprofessional—A term used to designate library employees without formal professional training/certification and who perform support and clerical duties.

Provisional certificate—A temporary one-year certificate issued to candidates who have not met requirements for an official license.

Qualitative standards—Recommendations based on levels of proficiency.

Quantitative standards—Recommendations based on numerical data.

Reading Counts—Computerized reading management program produced by Scholastic. Students can choose from 23,000 titles and take a short quiz afterward to verify comprehension.

Robin Hood Foundation—A private foundation that seeks to end poverty in New York City and currently is funding an initiative to renovate library media centers in New York City elementary schools.

Rubric—A set of established criteria, usually with levels of proficiency and point values, often used to evaluate and assess student work or aspects of school library media program quality.

School library media specialist—*See* library media specialist.

Shared library—*See* combined school-public library.

Single-track schedule—A method of scheduling students in year-round schools where the school operates with only one year-round calendar. All are students are in school and on vacation at the same time.

Site-based management—(SBM) A strategy that transfers significant decision-making authority from state and district offices to individual schools. It provides principals, teachers, students, and parents greater control over the education process by giving them responsibility for decisions about the budget, personnel, and the curriculum.

Standards—Principles or guidelines used to assess level of quality of service, material, facilities, and staff.

Technology coordinator—A staff person who is in charge of acquiring and maintaining computers and related peripherals for a school.

Weeding—The process of examining items in the library media program collection and identifying titles that will be permanently removed because the title is out-dated, in worn condition, or no longer relevant to the curriculum or to the needs of the school's students, teachers, staff, and community.

Index

10 reasons the Internet is no substitute for a library (Herring) 126

A

AASL
 See American Association of School Librarians
Absher, Linda 25
Academic libraries and librarians 5, 9, 111, 124, 130, 137

Accelerated Reader (Renaissance Learning Inc.). 73–82, 137

Access 64, 65, 66, 71, 86, 94, 97, 100, 101, 104, 106, 109, 120, 123, 126, 128, 129

24-7. 124
Accreditation 5, 7, 20, 137, 140
Acquisition 62, 137
Administrators. 12, 22, 28–29, 42, 45, 51, 54, 65, 68, 87, 93, 100, 105, 111, 112, 125
 See also Principals
Adobe Systems Incorporated. 128
AECT
 See Association for Educational Communications and Technology
ALA
 See American Library Association
Alabama staffing. 43
Alaska
 staffing 44
 Study. 35
Alt.support.shyness (Internet newsgroup) 26
American Association of School Librarians (AASL) 1, 2, 5, 12, 36, 50, 52, 53, 54, 55, 66, 87, 89, 123, 137

Access to resources and services in the school library media program 66
Directory of state and regional affiliate organizations 49
Mission statement 12
Position statement on appropriate staffing for school library media centers. 36–37
Position statement on flexible scheduling 84–85
Position statement on preparation of school library media specialists 1–2
Teaching for Learning Task Force Assessment Rubric Subcommittee 52
American Library Association (ALA). 1, 2, 5, 7, 22, 66, 137
 Freedom to Read statement 65
Arizona
 certification. 3
 staffing 44
Arkansas staffing 43
Askusquetions.com 124
Association for Educational Communications and Technology (AECT) 12, 50
Atalig, Kristi 107

B

Baker, Tim 23
Baker & Taylor 128
Ballinger, Charles E. 106
Bedminster Township School (New Jersey) 76
Berkeley Digital Library SunSITE. 124, 132, 135
Bertland, Linda 49
Best online graduate programs: Library science (U.S. News and World Report) 7, 17
Bickel, Jean 6
Big Bully. 23
Bishop, Kay. 61, 67, 70
Block scheduling
 See Scheduling—block
Book Adventure. 73, 75, 79, 137
Bookstores 100, 108–109, 113, 127
Book talk. 88, 108, 138
Breakfast Club, The. 24
Buchanan, Carol 76
Buchanan, Jan. 86
Buffy the Vampire Slayer 24–25
Burek Pierce, Jennifer 129

C

California
    facilities 107–108
    staffing 38, 44
Carrie 24
Carter, Betty 75
Censorship 28, 62, 65–67, 69, 110
    handling complaints 67
Certification 1–6, 8, 10, 12, 15, 17, 27,
        30, 37, 39, 40, 50, 104, 138
    types 4
Christine 23
Circulation . . . 64, 76, 80, 92, 100, 107, 129

Clairol Herbal Essence 25
Classroom libraries
    See Collections, classroom
Climate 99, 138
Coatney, Sharon 4
Coffee shops 108–109
Coffman, Steve 108
Collaboration 12, 64, 83, 85–86,
        92, 93, 94

Collection development
    See Collections, school
        library media center
Collection development policy 62, 138
Collections, classroom 63–64
Collections, school library media
    center 61–68
    computerized reading management
        programs and 76–77
    funding for 67–68
    popular materials and 64–65
    procedures associated with developing
        and maintaining 61–62
    selection of 62–63
    support of the curriculum 64–65
Color 112, 138
Colorado
    staffing 44
    Study 36
    Virtual Library 119
Combined scheduling
    See Scheduling—combined
Combined school-public
    libraries 100, 103–106, 138
Computer labs 93, 123, 129
Computerized reading management
    programs 73–82, 138
    budgets, effect on 76–77
    cheating and 74
    collections, effect on 76

    features 73–74
    motivation and 74–76
    research 77–78
    rewards and 74–76
Connecticut Digital Library (iCONN)
    Resources for Schools 124–125
Connecticut staffing 44
Corcoran, K. 108
Curriculum consultation 85

D

DeCandido, GraceAnne A. 24–25
Delaware staffing 44
Desk Set 21, 31
Despines, Janine 101–102
Dewalt, Mark W. 76
DeWitt Wallace Reader's
    Digest Fund 86, 99, 140
Digital divide 123, 131, 138
Digital libraries
    See Virtual School Libraries
Distance learning 7–9, 138
    considerations 7–8
    pros and cons 8–9
District library media director 37
District of Columbia
    budget 67
    staffing 43

E

eBooks 126–128, 130, 132, 138
Education
    school library media
        specialists' 1–20, 22,
        27–28, 30, 45
Educational Media Association of
    New Jersey (EMAnj) 100–101
Educational Testing Service (ETS) 3
E-global library 122
Eisenberg, Michael 9, 11–14
Electronic books
    See eBooks
Electronic books in libraries
    (Gibbons) 128
Electronic resources . . 7, 41, 51, 61, 68, 70,
        121–122, 125, 131, 139
    measuring use 129–130
EMAnj
    See Educational Media Association
        of New Jersey
Emergency certificate 4, 138
Endorsement 3, 139
Ergonomics 111, 117, 139
Everhart, Nancy L. . . . 4, 37, 39, 43–44, 52,
        73, 74, 75, 129–130, 150

Examination for certification of educators in Texas (ExCET)...... 3–4
Examining student work 130
Executive summary: Findings from the evaluation of the National Library Power program (DeWitt Wallace Reader's Digest Fund) 86
Extended hours
  See Facilities—Extended hours of
Extrinsic motivation.......... 74–76, 139

F

Facilities (school library media center) 29, 35, 36, 37, 99–117
  bookstores and............ 108–109
  extended hours of 101–102, 139
  necessity of 100–101
Farmer, Lesley S.J. 91–92
Fill rate 129
Flexible access library media programs (Buchanan) 86
Fitzgerald, Sara 40–41
Fixed scheduling
  See Scheduling—fixed
Flexible scheduling
  See Scheduling—flexible
Florida
  certification.................. 3, 5
  funding 102
  staffing 44
Follett Software Company........... 128
Formative assessment of reading comprehension by computer: Advantages and disadvantages of The Accelerated Reader (Topping).................... 78
Funding (for school library media center collections)
  See Collections, school library media center—funding for
Furnishings 51, 111–112, 138

G

Georgia staffing 44
Getting certified in 50 states: The latest requirements for school librarians (Perritt) 2–3
Gibbons, Susan.................... 128
Gierke, Carolyn 91–92
Giles, Rupert (*Buffy the Vampire Slayer*)...................... 24–25
Glick, Andrea........ 3–4, 38, 52, 53, 102
Guidelines
  See Standards

H

Hartzell, Gary 28–29, 53–54
Hawaii
  staffing 43
  University of .... vii, 106
  year-round schools 106–107
Heartland Area Education Agency..... 107
Herring, Mark 125–126
Homeschooled children
  See Homeschooling
Homeschooling 109–110, 114, 139
Homestead High School library (Cupertino, California) 108
Honda Accord..................... 25
Hughes-Hassell, Sandra........... 86–87

I

Idaho staffing 44
Illinois
  staffing 44
  University of.................. 7
Image of librarians resources (Internet Public Library) 23
Image of librarians 21–34
  advertising and........... 22–23, 25
  education and............... 27–28
  movies and................ 23–24
  school library media specialists' 22, 27–29
  stereotypes and 24, 26–27
  television and............... 24–25
  Web sites and 23
Indiana staffing..................... 44
Information literacy 10, 49, 52, 54, 63, 83, 86, 88, 123, 130
Information power: Building partnerships for learning (AASL/AECT) 12, 37, 39, 50, 52, 54–55, 57, 63, 84, 85
  criticism of 55
  flexible scheduling.............. 84
  Information literacy standards for student learning,...... 52, 86
Inside the digital divide: Connecting youth to opportunities in the new economy (Pearlman) 123
International Association of School Librarianship 27, 139
  Concord School Library Web Page Award 120
Internet 8, 22, 25–26, 41, 63, 68, 101, 121, 123–126
Internet and American Life (Pew Research Center)...... 121–122
Internet Public Library 23

Intrinsic motivation 74–75, 139
Invisible library 120–121, 139
Invisible school librarian: Why other educators are blind to your value, The (Hartzell) 28–29
Iowa staffing 43
It's a wonderful life 21
It's good to be inflexible (Johnson). . . 87–89

J

Jenkins, Christine 7
Job security 39, 42, 89
Johnson, Doug 38, 53, 87–89, 94
Joint-use libraries
  See Combined school–public libraries

K

Kansas staffing 43
Katz, Bill 13
Kellogg's Corn Flakes 25
Kennedy, Mike 112
Kentucky staffing 43
Kirschenman, Jean 92
Kohn, Alfie. 75
Krashen, Stephen. 65, 70, 102

L

Lance, Keith Curry 35–36, 102
Lau, Debra 1, 41, 100
Lehman, Kathy 120–121
Lenhart, Amanda 121–122
Librarian's guide to homeschooling resources, The (Scheps) 110
Librarians in the movies: An annotated filmography (Rarish) 23–24
Libraristic links: Librarians on parade (Smith). 25–26
Library Power 85–86, 99, 140
Lipstick librarian, The (Absher). 25
LM-NET 8–9, 40, 64, 110, 140
Louisiana staffing 43

M

Madden, Susan B. 110
Maine staffing. 44
Mandates   37–40, 42, 43–44, 45, 51, 52, 53, 56, 86, 88, 123, 140
Mansfield University. 7
Maryland
  budget 67–68
  staffing 44
Massachusetts
  staffing 44
  standards and guidelines 50
Massachusetts School Library Media Association Professional Standards Committee. 50

Master's degree. 1, 2, 3, 5, 6, 12, 26, 27, 104
McClure, Charles 129
McKracken, Anne 84, 85
Michigan staffing 44
Milbury, Peter 120
Miller, Marilyn L. 68, 77
Minkel, Walter 111
Minnesota
  staffing 38, 44
  standards and guidelines 53
Mississippi
  certification. 3
  staffing 39, 43
Missouri
  certification. 3
  staffing 43
M.L.S. (Master of Library Science). 1, 6, 140
Montana staffing. 43
Multi-track schedule (in year-round schools) 106–107, 140
Music Man, The 21

N

National Board for Professional Teaching Standards (NBPTS) 4
National Council for Accreditation of Teacher Education (NCATE) 2, 5, 140
National Council of Teachers of English 66
National Education Commission on Time and Learning 84
NBPTS
  See National Board for Professional Teaching Standards
NCATE
  See National Council for Accreditation of Teacher Education
Nebraska staffing 43
Nevada staffing. 44
New Hampshire staffing 43
New Jersey 76, 100
  certification. 3
  staffing 43
New Mexico staffing. 44
New York (New York)
  classroom libraries and 64
  facilities (school library media center) 99
New York
  certification. 5
  staffing 44, 50
  standards and guidelines 50, 52
North Carolina staffing 43

North Dakota
  certification 3, 5
  staffing 43
Nunn, Donna. 93

O

Observation 129–130
O'Dell, Charli 109
Ohio 124
  staffing 44
Oklahoma staffing 39, 43
Olson, Renee. 52–53
Online library degrees
  See Distance learning
*Open letter to Dr. Keith Swigger
  regarding his piece in
  "School Library Journal," An*
  (Eisenberg) 11–14
Oregon staffing 43
Our image: How they're seeing us 22

P

Palm OS 127–128
Paraprofessional 40, 140
Parks, Dee. 29
Party Girl 21–22
Pay raises 5
Peak, Jamie 76
Pearlman, Bob. 123
Pennsylvania 120
  staffing 39, 44
  Study 36
Perritt, Patsy 2–3, 4, 17
*Peter Milbury's network of school
  librarian web pages* 120
Pew Research Center 121–122
Pocket PC 128
Popular materials
  See Collections, school library media
  center, popular materials
Praxis II (Educational Testing Service) . . . 3
Prime of Miss Jean Brodie, The 23–24
Principals 28, 38, 39, 54, 56,
  67, 75, 79, 85, 125
  See also Administrators
Prisoners of time (National Education
  Commission on Time and
  Learning). 84
Prizes 75–77
Professionalization of school
  librarianship 10–12, 16
Professional organizations 49, 139
Provisional certificate 4, 140
Public libraries and
  librarians 9, 65, 100, 101, 102,
  103–106, 108, 109,
  110, 124, 129, 139

Public relations 29, 31

Q

Qualitative standards
  See Standards—qualitative
Quantitative standards
  See Standards—quantitative

R

Rarish, Martin 22, 23
Reading Counts
  (Scholastic) . . . 73, 74, 75, 77, 80, 141
Reading programs, computerized
  See Computerized reading
  management programs
Reitz, Joan M. 119
Renaissance Learning Inc. . . 73, 76–78, 137
  See also Accelerated Reader
Reports 73, 76, 77, 129
Rewards 74–77, 79, 137, 139
  See also Extrinsic motivation;
  Intrinsic motivation
Rhode Island staffing 43
Robin Hood Foundation. 99–100, 141
Roscello, Frances 50, 54
Role of the librarian in the digital
  age, The (E-global library). 122
Rome Adventure 24
Rubric 50, 52, 54, 130, 141

S

Sager, Don. 103–104
Saye, Jerry D. 26
Saturn (automobile). 25
Scheduling 83–98
  block 83, 84, 91–93, 94, 137
  combined 90–91, 94
  fixed 42, 83, 84, 85, 87–90, 90
  flexible 42, 53, 83, 84–87, 88,
  89, 90, 94, 139, 140
Scheps, Susan G. 110
Scholastic 73, 141
  See also Reading Counts
School library media centers
  necessity of 100–101, 125–126
  year-round schools
  and 106–107, 113, 140, 141
  See also Facilities
Selection (of school library media center
  materials) 41, 61–72, 111
  censorship and 65–67
  computerized reading management
  programs and 76–77
  policies 62, 67, 138
  responsibility for 62–63
Series books 65

Shared libraries
　See Combined school-public libraries
Shontz, Marilyn L. 68, 77
Simon, Jennifer. 107
Single-track schedule (in year-
　round schools) 106–107, 141
Site-based management 38, 41, 141
Smith, Bruce. 25
South Carolina staffing 43
South Dakota staffing 43
Springfield Township High School
　Virtual Library
　(Erdenheim, Pennsylvania) 120
Staff development 41, 93
Staffing 35–48, 50, 52–53, 100,
　　　　　　　　　　　102, 104, 105, 106
　shortages 39
　technology and. 40–42
　See also Mandates, Paraprofessionals,
　　Technology coordinators or
　　specialists
Standards 12, 49–59, 87, 141
　authority of 52–53
　communicating and
　　publicizing 53–54
　criticism of 55
　qualitative 51–52, 141
　quantitative 51–52, 141
　realism of 54–55
　reporting violations 53
State departments of
　education 2, 3, 7, 8, 49, 120
State digital libraries 124–125
State mandate for school library
　media specialists with ratios
　of students per school library
　media specialist (Figure 1). 43–44
State pages relating to school library/
　media services (Bertland) 49, 57
Stereotypes of librarians and school
　library media specialists
　See Image—stereotypes
Stevens, Norman. 21
Swigger, Keith. 9–11, 16, 55

T

Tallman, Julie I. 85
Teachers 2–3, 4, 6, 9–11, 12, 14, 22,
　　　　　　26, 28–29, 35, 36, 37, 38, 39, 40,
　　　　　　41, 42, 46, 53, 63, 66, 67, 70, 73,
　　　　　　75, 78, 83, 99, 100, 102, 107,
　　　　　　110, 114, 120, 121, 123
　Internet and 121, 123
　scheduling and. 85–94
　See also Collaboration; Staff
　　development

Teaching role of the school library
　media specialist 10–11, 41
Technology 40–42, 63, 67–68, 88,
　　　　　　　　　　110, 111, 123, 124, 128
　coordinator or
　　specialist. 37, 40–42, 45, 141
　See also Computerized reading
　　management programs,
　　Distance learning, eBooks,
　　Electronic resources, Internet,
　　Staffing—technology and
Teger, Nancy L. 93
Tennessee staffing. 43
Test scores 36, 55, 74, 77–78, 80
Texas
　certification. 3–4
　staffing 44
　standards and guidelines . . . 51, 52, 53
　State Library & Archives
　　Commission. 51
　Women's University 9, 11, 75
Thomas Dale High School
　(Chesterfield, Virginia). 120–121
Time, staff. 74, 77
Topping, Keith 78
Trejos, Nancy 87

U

United States Department of
　Education 124
　See also Virtual Reference Desk
　　Learning Center for Kids, The
U.S. News and World Report 7, 17
Utah staffing. 44

V

Valenza, Joyce 120, 121
Van Deusen, Jean Donham 85
Van Orden, Phyllis J. 61–62, 67, 70
Vermont staffing 43
Virginia staffing 44
Virtual Reference Desk Learning
　Center for Kids, The 124
Virtual school libraries. 119–136
　accessing 123–124
　role of 120–123
　school library media
　　specialist and 120–123
　See also State digital libraries

W

Washington(state)
　staffing 44
　University of 9, 12, 15
Washington, D.C.
　See District of Columbia

Weeding............... 62, 64, 138, 141
West Virginia staffing 44
What do you say when...: Talking points suggested responses for frequently asked questions
 (EMAnj) 100–101
What if you ran your library like a
 bookstore? (Coffman) 108
Whelock, Anne 86–87
Wisconsin
    certification.................... 5
    Department of Public
        Instruction 104–106
    staffing 43
Wisser, Katherine M.................. 26
Woolls, Blanche.............. 27–28, 51
Workstations, computer............. 111
Wyoming staffing 44

Y

Year-round schools 100, 106–107,
                      113, 140, 141

About the Author

Nancy Everhart, Ph.D. is an associate professor and coordinator of the school library media program at St. John's University, New York City. She is the recipient of numerous awards in the field of school librarianship. As a researcher she is the winner of the Association for Library and Information Science Education's Outstanding Dissertation Award and the Association of Specialized and Cooperative Library Agencies Research Award. As a school library media specialist she and her program won the Follett Microcomputer in the Media Center Award, the United States Department of Education's Outstanding Library Media Program, and Apple Computer's Merit Award. Author of *Evaluating the School Library Media Center* and over 50 journal articles, she serves as an associate editor for *School Library Media Research* and *Knowledge Quest*.

www.ingramcontent.com/pod-product-compliance
Lightning Source LLC
Chambersburg PA
CBHW070302010526
44108CB00039B/1646